and Merchant Queens

in Africa

OHIO SHORT HISTORIES OF AFRICA

This series of Ohio Short Histories of Africa is meant for those who are looking for a brief but lively introduction to a wide range of topics in African history, politics, and biography, written by some of the leading experts in their fields.

Female Monarchs and Merchant Queens in Africa

Nwando Achebe

OHIO UNIVERSITY PRESS

ATHENS

Ohio University Press, Athens, Ohio 45701
ohioswallow.com
© 2020 by Ohio University Press
All rights reserved
Printed in the United States of America
Ohio University Press books are printed on acid-free paper ⊚ ™
30 29 28 27 26 25 24 23 22 21 20 5 4 3 2 1

Front cover art and design by Adonis Durado.
www.adonisdurado.com

Library of Congress Cataloging-in-Publication Data

Names: Achebe, Nwando, 1970- author.
Title: Female monarchs and merchant queens in Africa / Nwando Achebe.
Other titles: Ohio short histories of Africa.
Description: Athens, Ohio : Ohio University Press, 2020. | Series: Ohio
   short histories of Africa | Includes bibliographical references and
   index.
Identifiers: LCCN 2020002540 | ISBN 9780821424070 (paperback) | ISBN
   9780821440803 (pdf)
Subjects: LCSH: Women--Africa--Social conditions. | Women heads of
   state--Africa. | Queens--Africa. | Women civic leaders--Africa. |
   Goddesses, African. | Power (Social sciences)--Africa.
Classification: LCC HQ1787 .A247 2020 | DDC 305.42096--dc23
LC record available at https://lccn.loc.gov/2020002540

To my husband, Folu Ogundimu,

For your unconditional love, support, and friendship,

This book is affectionately dedicated to you

Contents

Illustrations

Preface

Until Lions Have Their Own Historians,
the Story of the Hunt Will Always
Glorify the Hunter—Africanizing History,
Feminizing Knowledge

Whose histories, whose stories, whose archives? Almost six decades ago, Africanist historian Terence Ranger pondered the question of to what degree African history was actually truly African, and whether the methods and concerns derived from Western historiography were in fact sufficient tools for researching and narrating African history. This issue remains a foremost concern of many African-born researchers such as myself, who continue to question the manner in which African worlds have historically and contemporarily been (re)constructed.

We are cognizant of the fact that Africa was the site of some of the worst external abuses, a reality which resulted in a production of knowledge that has almost exclusively been shaped by these influences. We also share concerns regarding the ability of Africans to tell their own stories, on their own terms, free from Eurocentric biases. We are especially concerned about this because the inconceivable and arbitrary violence born out of slavery and colonial discourse has produced an African canon that is as dehumanizing and silencing as brute force.

From Muslim traders and travelers of the seventh to fifteenth centuries documenting African worlds in their travel logs to the accounts of European and Arab slavers, travelers, missionaries, and colonialists writing African worlds during the age of exploration, international slave trades, and conquest, these narratives have survived in what the eighth king of Dahomey, King Agonglo, described in 1793 as "books that never die," chronicling historical perspectives that were variously skewed, incomplete, and/or ethnocentric in their leanings. It is these narratives that have propelled the very nature of Africanist scholarship in the present day. Again, I ask, whose stories, whose histories, whose archives?

Given this historical reality, I have responded to the challenge of Africanizing and feminizing knowledge by attempting to restore voice and dignity to a people beset with memories of having been reduced to objects by slavers and colonial oppressors. I have done this by (re)framing and (re)telling the African gendered narrative in solidly African-centered and gendered terms. The end result is a body of scholarship—six monographs and a slew of journal articles and book chapters—that is unapologetically African-centered.

I have not rested easy with simply writing back at the received African canon. I have also, for the past twenty-five years, dedicated my career to honing my teaching of African history in the US college classroom. At Michigan State University, I have developed and taught several award-winning undergraduate-level courses on Africa, courses in which I have disseminated African-centered knowledge about Africa to thousands of young and inquiring minds.

In this context, I see myself as a missionary in reverse: one whose job it is to teach African worlds on their own terms; a person whose job it is to teach Africa in ways that Africans themselves conceptualize their histories and their worlds. And the end result of this pedagogical odyssey are histories that do not always neatly fit into Western-defined models of historical writing, understanding, and interpretation. Take for instance the fact that Africans do not necessarily conceptualize their histories in exclusively linear and strictly chronological terms. The proof of this can be found when a researcher approaches a living African archive, an African elder, with the following clear-sighted questions: "What year did a particular event occur?" or "How old are you?" These questions may seem simple and straightforward, and thus could be expected to elicit simple and straightforward answers. But, no sooner does the elder respond that he or she does not know what year the incident happened—or, worse still, shares with said researcher that he or she is about one hundred and fifty years old—than said researcher realizes that he or she has not asked the right questions. The right questions, the African-informed questions, should not be "In what year did a particular event occur?" or "How old are you?" They instead should be framed to discern what might have been happening historically around the time of the event or the elder's birth. Questions such as these would be sure to elicit more precise answers, answers such as the following: "The event occurred when daytime became nighttime" (read: during the coming of the locusts); or "I was born during the time of the great destroyer" (read: during the Great Influenza). Again, I ask, whose questions? Whose archives? Whose answers? For informed inquiry elicits informed answers and interpretations.

I teach what I describe to my students as the history of "Another Africa," an Africa that they most likely will not find in the average run-of-the-mill textbook. But it *is* the Africa that I know intimately, that I breathe, that I love. It *is* the Africa of my mother, grandmother, and all the African women who have, during my past twenty-five years of researching and writing African gendered worlds, entrusted me with their stories. It *is* an African history that continental Africans recognize and see themselves in. These *are our* histories, *our* stories, *our* archives.

Acknowledgments

I agreed to write this book at a time when my world had fallen apart. It was early 2013, and my dearest father, confidant, and friend, Chinua Achebe, had just passed away. It would be an understatement to say that I was not in the frame of mind to begin the process of researching and writing these African women's worlds; it would take me the better part of five years to get to a point where I had healed sufficiently to put pen to paper.

I would like to thank Gill Berchowitz for realizing that I was in a very bad place when I had committed to this project. For not pressuring me after I had missed the submissions deadline by more than four years, for continuing to believe in me and my ability to pull this project together, Gill, heartfelt thanks are not enough. Thus, in the tongue of my foremothers, I say, *dalu so.*

During the course of writing this small book, things would again fall apart in my world, as the love of my life, my greatest cheerleader and supporter, my spouse, Folu Ogundimu, was facing a life without sight. He would give me the strength to persevere and see this project through. For that I am eternally grateful and dedicate this effort to him.

I would also like to thank Tara Reylets, James Blackwell, Chioma Uchefuna, and Eric Kesse, who served as graduate assistant researchers for me. Their help in locating source material for this book is very much appreciated. Thanks also go to Harry Odamtten and Peter Alegi, who provided Asante-Twi and isiZulu translations.

My heartfelt thanks extend to the two anonymous reviewers who read this manuscript closely and provided comments and suggestions for improvement. To Rick S. Huard, acquisitions editor of Ohio University Press, I say another *dalu so,* for his steadfast support and encouragement of my vision for this project.

I would be remiss if I did not acknowledge the love and support of my family and friends. Immeasurable thanks go to my mother, Professor Christie Chinwe Achebe, whose love and support have been a constant in my life. She has had faith in me, even when I have not. She has carried me when I have faltered. She is my rock. My daughter, Chino, my heart, my life. I have watched you grow into a beautiful, intelligent, and poised woman; I hope you find inspiration in the lives and worlds of these powerful and influential African women. Last, but not least, my friends Pero Dagbovie and LaShawn Harris, Melissa McDaniels, Carl Taylor, Dee Jordan, Dawne Curry, Deborah Johnson, Dave and Lorraine Weatherspoon, Shawna Forester, Linda Kahler, and Philip Effiong deserve special mention. Each has been an attentive and supportive ear for me during this difficult past year and a half. Thank you, thank you, thank you.

I hope that this book serves to introduce my readers to the fascinating and compelling worlds of elite African women. As an African woman myself, I can attest to the fact that these [her]stories of powerful and influential African women, and the female principle, give me a sense of pride in whence I have come, and who I am.

Introduction

The Preamble

In a 2014 newspaper story, "Women Arrest Boko Haram Fighters in Borno," Hausa journalist Hamza Idris reports on a mysterious incident that throws light on the conviction held by African peoples about the interconnectedness of the human and spiritual worlds, and the forces therein.[1] Illustrating the belief in the ability of human beings to tap into this unseen world of spirits and channel their extraordinary powers to influence activity in the visible human world, the article captures the interconnectivity between the two worlds:

> Some women in Gwoza town of Borno State are said
> to have arrested seven Boko Haram[2] fighters who
> wreaked havoc in the town on Sunday. Shortly after
> their arrest[,] angry youth and vigilantes in the town
> rallied and lynched [the terrorists]. . . . Some residents
> who spoke to *Daily Trust attributed the daring arrest by
> the women [to] mystical powers.* Sources in Gwoza said
> many insurgents had earlier in the day intercepted

a vehicle loaded with bread, slaughtered four of the occupants[,] and drove the vehicle towards Sambisa Forest.... A witness from Gwoza, who did not want his name mentioned, said, "After seizing the vehicle conveying the bread and other valuables in Gwoza ... some of the insurgents moved towards the Sambisa (Forest) and met some women on the way[:] *"The insurgents wanted to attack the women but their guns did not work. They tried hitting them with the boot [sic] of their guns but mysteriously, all the hands of the insurgents hung* until youth and vigilantes in the area mobilized and killed them." ... Mohammed Gava, the chairman of local vigilantes in Borno State[,] confirmed the incident[:] "When the gunmen were moving out of Gwoza, most people fled to safety but those women refused to flee. I think the insurgents were angry and wanted to attack them but met their waterloo."[3]

Ascribing the women's brazen arrest of the Boko Haram terrorists to "mystical powers," directed by these women, to paralyze the insurgent's guns and immobilize their hands is an attribution that reads true for the over three thousand nations of people who inhabit the African continent. It is this belief in the interconnectedness between the human and spiritual worlds and in the viability of power flowing from spirits to humans that we witness in the explanation of the Gwoza women's action. And it is these various elucidations, conceptualized from an African-centered perspective, about the ways in which African women and/or the female spiritual principle exhibit power, influence, and authority that *Female Monarchs and Merchant Queens in Africa* seeks to highlight.

Methods, Focus, and Definitions

One of the central features of African historiography has been the fact that Africans produced fewer documents that historians have traditionally considered to be "evidence"—government reports, letters, diaries, travel logs, wills, and property records. This has meant that until recently the voices and the worldview of Africans were completely excluded from major works of African history—a fact compounded in reconstructions of African women and gendered worlds.

With limited access to the traditional sources that scholars typically use to document their work, African-centered gender historians have necessarily had to find new methods to explore the voices of people who have historically been denied a voice. This text is part of that intellectual odyssey, functioning as a corrective while utilizing, where available, African-derived sources, including language/linguistics, the meaning and significance of names, metaphors, symbolism, cosmology, chronicles, songs, folktales, proverbs, oral traditions, and traditions of creation, to record the worldview and experiences of African women who did not leave written evidence of their lives in their own voices.

Regrettably, this African-/gendered-centered source material is not evenly or consistently distributed across the continent. Thus, this narrative, in places, may seem to privilege one African region—for instance, the privileging of West Africa in the "Merchant Queens" chapter—over some others. When documenting early African women and gendered worlds, this lacuna is further amplified by an unevenness of available source material across time and space, resulting in histories that may appear incomplete and regionally fractured or unbalanced.

The chapters within this book have been thematically and roughly chronologically organized, with reference to regional space and time. When and wherever possible, I have sought to establish sustained change over time within reconstructions of particularized narratives. However, due to the regional- and time-specific porosity of certain source material, this has not always been possible. Thus, in those instances, I work to establish change over time by reading and analyzing one regionally based and time-defined case study against another, and in the process, pooling to completeness, an overall historical narrative.

While paying homage to the diversity of lived experience on so vast a continent, I have necessarily, in this short history, had to generalize certain African gendered realities that read true across regions and periods. I have done this not to be reductionist about the complexities of African realities but rather to present an overall narrative that is uncompromised in its accessibility and scope.

From Amma[4] to *inkosazana*,[5] Sobekneferu[6] to Nzingha,[7] Nehanda[8] to Ahebi Ugbabe,[9] the *kandake*s of Meroë[10] to Omu Okwei,[11] and the daughters or *umuada* of Igboland, *Female Monarchs and Merchant Queens in Africa* documents the worlds and life histories of elite African females, female principles, and (wo)men of privilege. It centers the diverse forms and systems of leadership, as well as complexities of female power at the highest level, in a multiplicity of distinct African societies.

I use the terms "female principle" and "female spiritual principle" to speak to—and give voice to—the totality of leadership and authoritative roles occupied by female entities in Africa. These terms are inclusive and speak to the manifestations of all dimensions of femaleness in society, be they in the human, seen, world (female principle) or the spiritual, unseen, world (female spiritual principle). In the human world, the female principle is embodied in women's roles as overseers and females of privilege, including women leaders of their people or wives of male leaders. These women exercise great power, authority, and influence publicly, temporally, and in spiritual/religious spheres. My focus on the female spiritual principle (i.e., female spiritual monarchs like rain queens, spirit mediums, priestesses, goddesses, masked spirits, *sangomas, female* medicines, and prophetesses) is informed by African cosmology, which recognizes the existence of two distinct but interconnected worlds—the human visible or physical world,

23

and the more powerful and commanding spiritual invisible world. This understanding consequently allows me to underscore the power, influence, and authority of the African Great God, a spiritual force that in most African cosmological reasoning inhabits a space that is neither male nor female but is essentially a balance of male and female forces, male and female principles.

The terms "African females" and "(wo)men" also encourage an investigation into the place and power of gendered females and males in African societies. These "gendered females" include biological males who transform themselves into women. "Gendered males" include biological females or (wo)men who transform themselves into men. These transformations are encouraged by a milieu that recognizes that biological sex and gender do not coincide; that gender is a social construct and is flexible and fluid, allowing biological women to become gendered men, and biological men, gendered women. This phenomenon gives rise to distinctive African categories such as female husband, male priestess, female headman, female king, and female pharaoh.

In political matters (chapters 1 and 2), as in African cosmology, Africans recognize two political constituencies—the human and the spiritual. The gods and goddesses, or put differently, spiritual monarchs, were the real rulers of African communities and towns, and human beings were merely there to interpret the will of the spirits.[12] These spiritual monarchs occupied the spiritual political constituency and wielded supernatural power in the human world over human beings. Conversely, the female principle of (wo)men leaders, including queens, queen mothers, princesses, merchant queens, and *female* kings, are highlighted in my discussion of African (wo)men's leadership roles in the human political constituency. Throughout the narrative, the connection between African worlds and political constituencies is documented.

In economic matters (chapter 3), African women owned the marketplace. They controlled it and defined its rules and regulations. The marketplace, although physically located in the human world, is connected, in important ways, to the spiritual world, in the sense that most African markets have a market deity in charge of the market. Thus, whether African women engage in local or long-distance trade, pottery making, weaving, or farming, the most accomplished of these women, otherwise known as merchant or market queens, understand, nurture, and subsume the power inherent in upholding the interconnectedness between the physical and spiritual worlds, often translating these connections into powerful expressions of economic power.

Let me now say a word or two about my conceptualization of power, influence, and authority. What are the differences among them? In this book, I use the term "power" to mean the capacity or ability to direct or influence the behavior of others or the course of events. "Influence" means the capacity to have an effect on the character, development, or behavior of someone or something. And "authority" means the power or right to give orders, make decisions, and enforce obedience. It is my contention that African females, (wo)men, and the female spiritual principle have always held power, influence, and authority. And it is the myriad ways in which the totality of elite African (fe)male expression and manifestation has held power, influence, and authority that is the subject of this book.

The African Worldview: A Case for African Centeredness and Balance

> Where one thing stands, something else will stand beside it.
>
> —Igbo proverb

The African world is a world of dualities. African people identify two worlds: The human or physical/visible world is made up of the heavens, earth, and waters. It is the world of human beings and of natural forces and phenomena. The nonhuman or spiritual/invisible world is a world of divine beings, of good and bad spirits, and of departed ancestors. It is the unseen world, the world that we cannot see. These worlds are not separate, but like two halves of a kola nut, they are connected, and make up one continuous, complete, and whole African world. The visible and invisible worlds commune and interact with each other.

The African world is cyclical. This is why most Africans believe in reincarnation—the never-ending cycle

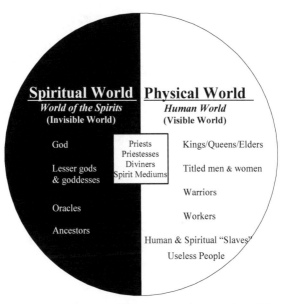

Figure I.1. The African worldview. Diagram by Nwando Achebe.

of life. A person is born, grows old, dies, and is reborn, and the cycle continues. The pouring of libation to the ancestors in Africa symbolizes the establishment of a connection between the physical human world (where libation is poured) and the spiritual nonhuman world of ancestors and spirits who inhabit the bowels of the earth. Ancestors (the reborn) also appear in the human world during periods of crisis or celebration. They are able to influence the fortunes of the living. They appear as masked spirits who protect the society as community guards or police; as courts of arbitration, which provide binding spiritual justice in trials among human beings; or as entertainers, enthralling viewers with the beauty of the masquerade dance during celebratory periods in the life of the community, such as festivals.

Africans believe that the human and nonhuman worlds are too big to contemplate. They believe that there are spirits all around them. There are too many for one to even know; therefore, they have mediums to help explain the universe. These mediums—diviners, priests, priestesses, and spirit mediums—are special human beings. They are born into the human world but are endowed with spiritual abilities.

At the zenith of the spiritual world is God. The African God is neither male nor female (see chapter 1). God is a supernatural force that balances both male and female principles. There are as many African names for God as there are peoples—over three thousand. For instance, the Acholi of Uganda call God *Jok;* the Asante and Fante of Ghana and Côte d'Ivoire, *Nyame;* the Azande of Sudan, *Mbori* or *Mboli;* and the Lovedu of South Africa, *Mwari.*

God is too great to behold. Thus, She/He is assisted by a pantheon of more accessible lesser gods and goddesses. These lesser gods and goddesses are autonomous yet interdependent. They are personifications of natural phenomena. Their jurisdictions are localized. Africans have gods and goddess of land, lightning, thunder, streams, rivers, and so on. Some of these deities are neither totally male nor totally female but embody the duality of male and female forces that African cosmology so commonly elevates. For instance, the rainbow snake *ayida-weddo* god(dess) of the Fon people of Benin is believed to possess this balance of male (the red part of the rainbow) and female (the blue part of the rainbow) principles.

Oracles are forces that explain the past and predict the future. Like gods and goddesses, oracles can be either male or female. The word "oracle" derives from the Latin *orare* (to speak). Oracles, through their priests and priestesses, "speak" their predictions and explanations.

As alluded to earlier, priests, priestesses, diviners, and spirit mediums are human beings who have been endowed with spiritual abilities to decipher, interpret, and communicate the worlds of the spirits. In general, priests and priestesses are attached to a given deity and serve to articulate the pronouncements of that deity. African cosmology typically calls for a balancing of male and female principles in the relationships between mediums and spiritual forces. Thus, when there is a god, that god is most likely served by a priestess; and when there is a goddess, the goddess is most likely served by a priest. For instance, among the Igbo of Nigeria the goddess, *ani,* is served by the priest, *ezeani;* and the Egyptian goddess of fertility, nature, and animals, *serket,* is served by a priest. It is this same balance that is also witnessed in African constructions of the Great God as both male and female.

Diviners, unlike priests and priestesses, are not attached to particular deities. They are special human beings who work for society at large, casting beads or cowrie shells (Igbo and Yoruba of Nigeria) or copper lances (Burundi), practicing invocation (Nyole, Uganda), using baskets (BaKongo of Kongo), counting stars (Amhara of Ethiopia), evoking trances (Baule of Côte d'Ivoire), using animals (Zande, Kapsiki, and Higi of Cameroon; Baule), and consulting astrological and numerological texts (Swahili) to form, understand, and explain the present and to predict events in the future. They are inspired by a god or goddess to foresee, to gain insight into a question.

Spirit mediums are human beings who mediate communication between the spirits of the dead and human beings. They do this through actual possession, in a trance or spirit channeling. The spirit of the deceased speaks through these mediums, relaying important information and messages of support. Taken collectively, these special individuals that inhabit the in-between worlds are the human voices of the unseen world, a world that they explain to human beings.

The physical visible world is the world of human beings: men, women, and children. This world, like the spiritual world, is hierarchical, and depending on the kind of society—centralized or egalitarian—is led either by kings and queens, or male and female elders, in a dual-sex or complementary fashion. Women in Africa have authority and influence because of their own achievements, not those of their husbands. Thus, a queen or queen mother is powerful in her own right as a ruler, and not because she is married to a king or is his birth mother. In fact, queen mothers in the African system are not necessarily mothers of a sitting king.

Next in rank to these leaders of their societies are the titled men and women. Like the queens, queen mothers, or female elders, titled women are recognized for their own achievements and not those of their husbands. All African societies have male and female warriors, whose job it is to protect their societies from their enemies. The Amazons of Dahomey, an all-female regiment of warriors, who operated in the sixteenth through the nineteenth centuries, were particularly powerful and led their kingdom from victory to victory.

In Africa, all able-bodied individuals regardless of gender are expected to contribute to society by working outside their homes. African women have always worked, and can be seen, even today, carrying their babies on their backs while going back and forth between the farm and marketplace.

Indigenous "slavery" can be both empowering and disempowering for the enslaved. "Slavery" in Africa is not a permanent condition. Enslaved persons work for their masters, for a given period of time, after which they are able to manumit themselves and either stay in the community of their masters or find their way back to their natal communities. African "slaves" who are attached to the spiritual world either as wives, daughters, or sons of deities find their station in society elevated because of their relationship to the said deity. In many

ways, this relationship serves to empower them in rela-
tion to mere mortals.

At the very bottom of the physical world's hierarchy are useless people. These are able-bodied men and
women who refuse to work. They are deemed useless
because they are not contributing to society in mean-
ingful ways.

Chapter Outline

Female Monarchs and Merchant Queens in Africa
highlights the similarities and differences in (fe)male
leadership experiences in various geographical spaces,
times, and settings in Africa. From centralized to small-
scale egalitarian societies, patrilineal to matrilineal
systems, North Africa to Africa south of the Sahara, this
book provides an overview of a representative group of
remarkable African (wo)men and/or female spiritual
principles who occupied, and continue to occupy, positions of power, authority, and influence.

This introduction serves to place the authority, influence, and power of African women and the female
principle in proper context. What does it mean to be influential or powerful? Why is it important to frame our
conversations about female power, authority, and influence around realities in both the spiritual and the physical
worlds? This chapter presents these and other questions,
while setting up the trajectory of the rest of the book.

Chapter 1, "Spiritual Monarchs: God, Rain Queens,
Spirit Mediums, and Goddesses," locates the sources of

female spiritual and ritual power within various African communities. I also consider the ritual leadership of female gendered spiritual forces such as goddesses, oracles, and female medicines and their human helpers (e.g., priestesses, diviners, spirit mediums, and prophetesses). Case studies of Lovedu rain queens; Nyamwezi and Shona spirit mediums, including Nehanda; Igbo and Yoruba priestesses of gods, *male* priestesses of goddesses; and South African *sangomas* are highlighted.

Chapter 2, "Queens, Queen Mothers, Princesses, and Daughters," documents the lives and times of a representative sample of African princesses, queens, and queen mothers from different parts of Africa at different times, including queens Nefertiti of Egypt and Amina of Hausaland; queen mothers Labotsibeni Mdluli of Swaziland (now Eswatini) and Yaa Asantewa of Ejisu, Asanteland; and princesses Inikpi of the Igala Kingdom and Magogo of Zululand. These women exerted considerable influence over men's offices. It also documents the place that daughters in egalitarian societies occupy. The chapter poses the questions: To whom were these women accountable? On whose behalf did they exercise power?

African women were known for their economic acumen, and they often formed complex socioeconomic networks with other women and used these networks to empower themselves. Chapter 3, "Merchant Queens," explores the power and influence of women commodity leaders, association leaders, and leaders of market organizations, courts, and police forces. Case studies of West African merchant queens like Madam Efunroye Tinubu, Omu Okwei, other *Omus* (Nigeria), and market *ahemma* (Ghana) are highlighted. So are the life histories of some West African Mama or Nana Benzs.

Chapter 4, "*Female* Headmen, Kings, and Paramount Chiefs," highlights the flexibility and fluidity of the African gender system that allowed women to become men, and men, women. It does this through the lens of (fe)male leaders who transformed themselves into gendered males and achieved political power and clout, occupying positions that were traditionally regarded as male. The lives and times of *female* kings like Hatshepsut, who dressed and ruled as pharaoh; Ebulejonu, the first *female* king of the Igala monarchy; Headman Wangu wa Makeri of Gĩkũyũland, colonial Kenya; and Paramount Chief Mosadi Seboko of the Balete people of Botswana are highlighted.

Chapter 5, "African Women Today," brings the narrative of women's power, influence, and authority to the present. It does this by exploring women's leadership at the highest levels, be they presidents or vice presidents, legislators, senators, or ministers; high-profile women business entrepreneurs; or leaders of megachurches and in the Islamic faith.

1

Spiritual Monarchs

God, Goddesses, Spirit Mediums, and Rain Queens

The *modjadji* or rain queen of Lovedu, South Africa, is[1] believed to be the living embodiment of the rain goddess. She has special powers. Also referred to as the *Khifidola-maru-a-Daja* (transformer of clouds), the modjadji guarantees the seasonal cycle and controls the clouds, rainfall, and fertility of the crops. Like rain queens, spirit mediums are believed to be embodiments of the spirits or the ancestors. It is a form of possession in which a person serves as an intermediary between the gods and society. In hierarchical societies, such as the Nyamwezi, spirit medium societies provide women with the most-direct avenues for active participation in politics and religious life. Spirit mediums can achieve measures of power that place them above men and all mortals.

In African societies, deities, the most powerful of whom is the Great Creator God, serve as the true political heads or spiritual monarchs of their communities. Next in rank to God are the lesser gods and goddesses. Personifications of natural phenomena, the most influential are gendered females, deities in charge of the waters and the land. These deities are the moral judges of conduct and wield power indiscriminately.

Starting with the African Great Creator God, this chapter locates the sources of female/women's ritual and political power, which I refer to as the female spiritual political constituency, within various African communities. In the pages that follow, I center the leadership of (fe)male gendered spiritual forces such as goddesses, oracles, female medicines, and their human helpers (e.g., priestesses, diviners, spirit mediums, and prophetesses)—the *real* rulers of African kingdoms, paramounts, towns, and communities. I anchor my discussion in regional case studies that speak to the power, gender, and metaphor of God, the ultimate leader of the spiritual political constituency, and the power, authority, and influence of (fe)male lesser deities, rain queens, spirit mediums, priestesses of the gods, priests of the goddesses, and traditional medicine workers and healers. First, we must understand how African society is organized politically.

The Female Principle in African Politics: The Female Spiritual Political Constituency

In Africa, there are basically two political constituencies: the spiritual and the human. The spiritual political constituency is made up of divinities: male and female functionaries who derive their political power from an association with the spiritual world. These spiritual functionaries or leaders are organized in a hierarchical manner (see worldview diagram, figure I.1, in the introduction).

The human political constituency (see chapter 2) is made up of executives who achieve their political potential as human actors in the physical realm. The text that follows delves into the spiritual political constituency, starting with the most powerful of these spiritual entities, the African Great God.

The Power of God

African cosmological accounts submit that God is the origin of all things. All-knowing and all-powerful, Great or High God is the supreme being who created the world, nature, animals, and humans. The 512 nations that make up present-day Nigeria have descriptive names for God. The Igbo, for instance, call God *Chukwu,* which means "the Great One from whom beings originate." They also call God *Chineke,* "The Creator of all things." The Edo refer to God as *Osanobua* (or *Osanobwa*), meaning "the Source of all beings who carries and sustains the world or universe"; and the Nupe call God *Soko,* meaning "the Creator or Supreme Deity that resides in heaven." Other West African groups like the Mende of Sierra Leone also have descriptors for God. For them, God or *Ngewo* is "the Eternal One who rules from above."[2]

Ngai is the Supreme Being of the Gĩkũyũ, Maasai, and Kamba people of East Africa. Although Ngai's abode is in the sky, Ngai's special dwelling place on earth is the Kirinyaga mountain ranges; hence the Gĩkũyũ also refer to God as *Ngai wa Kirinyaga.* In Tanzania, there is no equal to the Ruanda people's Supreme Being *Imana.* The southern Sudanese Dinka call God *Nhailic* ("That which is above") or *Jok,* meaning "Spirit" or "Power." To the Nuer of Sudan, God is *Kwoth,* and Kwoth is not the sky, the moon, or the rain; Kwoth reveals Her-/Himself through these natural phenomena.[3]

Among the Batswana of southern Africa, God is *Modimo* (*Molimo*), meaning "One who dwells on high or the High One." Among the Zulu, Great God is called *uNkulunkulu,* meaning "Great, Great One" or "Old, Old, One." The Zulu regard God, also called *Mvelinqangi* (the First Out Comer), as the ancestor of all. Some southern African Nguni groups call God *Qamata* (The First One), and *Umdali* (Creator).[4] Among the Baila and Botanga of northern Zambia, God is known as *Leza* (the One who does what no other can do).

African peoples believe that God is eternal and immortal. One of the names that the Kono of Sierra Leone call God is *Meketa* (the Everlasting One).[5] God is also invisible, incomprehensible, mysterious, beyond understanding, and unpredictable. God may never be questioned or cursed. Radically transcendent and immanent, God is above and greater than all else. God is not limited to a particular place or time, God cannot be confined to heaven or earth. God is everywhere. God dwells among us and within us. The Kono of Sierra Leone express this reality in another one of the names that they give God, *Yataa,* meaning "God is the One you meet everywhere."[6]

In spite of these attributes, God is not usually worshipped directly, but is paid high respect. In some African nations, God does not have any priests or dedicated shrines, hence the intimation by some scholars that the African God is a distant God. This assessment is, however, simplistic and does not read entirely true. The African understanding of God is more complex and nuanced than mere binary classifications. In reality, God is distant, or separated from the affairs of human beings, only in the sense that God is perceived as being too big to behold by these humans, and therefore they cannot understand God. This paradoxical complementarity of the closeness yet distance of God is expressed by the Nupe in their conceptualization of God (Soko). They say, "God is far away. God is in front. God is in the back."[7]

The Gender of God in Africa: How God Became He

In the Judeo-Christian framework God is presented as male. In this Western patriarchal religious tradition, the female persona of God in Africa is suppressed. In addition, African theologians and scholars have attempted to prove that the European missionaries did *not* introduce the concept of God to the continent; thus, many of them equated the belief in an African Supreme God in all three thousand–plus nations in Africa to belief in a Christian God who is imagined as male. This assessment spilled over to their non-African counterparts, who in their writing and interpretations of God also necessarily adopted male pronouns and gender. P. J. Paris, a theologian specializing in African religion, for instance, argues that the African God is the same as the Christian God, who is regarded as the *father* of our Lord Jesus Christ, not His *mother*.[8]

The true conceptualization of God in Africa is actually much more nuanced, much more complex. In several African societies, the supreme divinity is neither male nor female. However, referring to God in English has been complicated by the fact that African languages do not have gender-specific pronouns—African pronouns are gender-neutral. This gender neutrality has however been lost when African names for God have been translated into European languages. The result is that the genderless African Creator God has been written about with the pronoun "He," a handicap that owes its origins to the gender-specific nature of these languages. In consequence, translations of African theology into the missionary/colonial languages of English, French, and Portuguese produced a discourse about God in Africa in which God became male.

The Metaphor of God

Nevertheless, African metaphors for God do not necessarily reflect the ways in which theologians or religious historians of Africa write about God. For the Zulu, Swati, Xhosa, Basotho, Batswana, Bapedi and Barotse, Shona, Kalnga, Ndau, Sena, Venda, Tsonga, Ihambane, Herero, and Ndebele, and the three thousand–plus peoples that inhabit the African continent, the names for

God are gender-neutral. Indeed, most African societies believe that the world was created by a genderless Creator God. Among the Diola of present-day Senegambia, the genderless Great God is called *Emitai.* The Igbo Great God of eastern Nigeria, *Chukwu* (or *Chineke*), is likewise neither male or female. The Ewe and Fon Creator Deity, *Mawu* (female) *Lisa* (male), exhibits both male and female qualities or principles. For the Ga of Ghana, *Ataa Naa Nyonmo* is a combination of *Ataa* (old man) and *Naa* (old woman). Thus, *Ataa Naa Nyonmo* translates into "Father Mother God."[9] The Akan also believe in a genderless God, *Kwasi Asi a daa Awisi* ("The Male-Female One").[10]

Some African societies regard their Creator God as female. For instance, the Creator God of the Tarakiri Ezon of the Niger Delta region of Nigeria, *Tamarau,* is considered female and her name means "our Mother." She is sometimes also called *Ayebau,* which means "the Mother of the world." For the Krobos of Ghana, God—*Kpetekplenye*—is also female. She is considered to be the "Mother of all big and wonderful things."[11] The southern Nuba, who have a matrilineal system of descent, also personify the Supreme God as female. According to comparative religious scholar Geoffrey Parrinder, "The southern Nuba . . . refer to God as 'the Great Mother' and when praying beside a dying person they say, 'Our God, who has brought us into this world, may *She* take you.'"[12]

Mwari is the most common name for God among the Shona of Southern Africa. The metaphors surrounding Mwari exist in closest association with the female principle. For instance, the metaphor for God most commonly used among the Shona is *Mbuya* (grandmother). The VaHera substitute *Mbuya* for *Mwari* when they refer to Mwari's powers of creation and fertility. *Runji* is another God as mother metaphor used to depict the Creator God. This Shona word means "needle," which, like lightning, metaphorically sews the heavens and earth together. The craft of sewing (*kusona*) among the Shona, moreover, is not only traditionally associated with women: all women are expected to know how to sew.[13]

The female image of God is also reflected in the Shona metaphor for God as *muvumbapasi* (molder or fashioner of things). Another popular metaphor used for God among the Shona is *musikavanhu.* This metaphor speaks to the fact that God is both male and female. Among the Shona, the word *kusika* is associated with the kindling of fire with two sticks. One of the sticks has a hole in it, in which grass is placed, and the other stick, *musika,* is twisted in the hole until fire is created. This fire-making tool symbolizes male and female organs.[14] The female image of God is also expressed in metaphors that depict God as *dziva/dzivaguru* and *chidziva chopo.* These metaphors associate God with water. Water is regarded by the Shona as a symbol for the universal mother, who is the source of all life. The Shona also have metaphors that clearly depict God as male. One is *sororezhou/wokumusoro.* S*ororezhou* means "elephant head" or father, and *wokumusoro* means "he who dwells on high." Thus, in Shonaland, God is both male and female.[15]

The Genderless or Dual-Gender African God

Among the Malagasy of Southern Africa, the Supreme God is *Zanahary* or *Andriamanitra.* The source of life, creator of all things, and the founding and primary ancestor of the Malagasy, Zanahary is believed to be both male and female. She/He is both celestial and terrestrial. The earthly Zanahary created humans from clay or wood, and the heavenly Zanahary breathed life into them. Zanahary is a supreme judge of moral justice. She/He judges *tangena*[16] ordeals and distinguishes between the innocent and the guilty. Zanahary also sees in the darkness as well as in the light.[17]

In the western part of the continent live the Diola of Casamance, who call the Great God *Emitai.* Emitai is both male and female. She/He is believed to have "made everything, even the little ants."[18] She/He is all-knowing, the provider of the necessities of life, and a source of aid in times of trouble. Emitai is closely associated with rain and fertility, She/He communicates with humans through dreams and visions and selects certain people to reveal Her/His moral teachings.[19]

The Dogon of Mali, neighbors of the Senegambia and the Diola, refer to the Creator God as *Amma.* Amma is the maker of the earth, life, fertility, and rain.[20] The word *amma,* like many African words, has more than one meaning. In addition to referencing the Dogon Supreme God, the word can also mean "to grasp, to hold firm, or to establish." The Dogon believe that Amma holds the world firmly in both hands. Although commonly written about as male, the metaphor of Amma as the God who gives life and fertility invokes the female principle. To this end, the Dogon consider Amma to symbolize both male and female principles. Amma is therefore more appropriately characterized as genderless or as being of dual gender.[21]

The Maasai, Embu, Meru, and Gĩkũyũ of Kenya call their genderless Great God *Ngai*. Ngai created the world and is sometimes referred to as female, as is suggested in the saying, "*Naamoni aiyai,*" which means "The She to whom I pray." Ngai manifests in two forms: *Ngai Narok,* the good and benevolent Ngai, who is represented as black; and *Ngai Na-nyokie,* the angry Ngai, who is represented as red. In neighboring Tanzania, among the Haya people their Great God, *Wamara,* rules the universe. Wamara is neither male or female, and Her/His role is not gender-specific. Wamara is supreme among all other deities and spirits and is the sovereign of the souls of the dead. Haya women play a central role in the worship of Wamara. The new moon sacrifice performed in Wamara's honor is marked by the gathering of the clan, and the offering of coffee beans, banana beer, and grass by the women.[22]

Whereas the vast majority of African groups describe a gradual formulation of the world or universe in stages, the ancient Egyptians reference a time before creation, a time before the appearance of land and light, during which four pairs of male and female forces emerged out of chaos. This is in agreement with the African belief in the importance of dualities and balance in their worlds. The male and female forces appeared simultaneously. *Nun* (m) and *nunet* (f) represented the watery expanse, and lack of solidity. They were the god and goddess of the ocean. *Heh* (m) and *hehet* (f) represented unending time, a lack of time. They were charged with raising the sun. *Kek* (m) and *keket* (f) represented darkness or a lack of light. Their mission was to produce the gloom of the night in which light would emerge. Finally, *tenem* or *amun* (m) and *tenemet* or *amaunet* (f) represented a lack of direction, wandering. They were the forces of mystery or the hidden. These eight forces that existed before creation, or the Hermopolitan Ogdoad, represent the Egyptian early stage of creation, which continued with the emergence of Ra and the first generation of deities.

Creation proper was then ordered by the ancient Egyptian principal Creator God, the Sun-God, *Ra.* Ra was also called *Atum, Atem,* or *Tem,* the "Complete One," who created, completed, or finished the world. This universal God of the Egyptians rules heaven, earth, and all other gods. Atum is connected to a pair of male and female forces: *Shu,* the air and moisture that carry the sky, and *Tefinut,* the female supplement of Shu. Shu and Tefinut are offshoots of Ra or Atum; they are expressions of Atum's function.[23] South of Egypt, in the land of the Nubians, the Great Creator God of the Shilluk people of Sudan is *Juok*. Juok is formless and invisible, and like air is believed to be everywhere. Juok is more powerful than any deity or human, and is worshipped through Nyakang, the first king and founder of the Shilluk nation.[24]

To summarize, the dual nature of God is consistent with the broader cosmological principles of numerous African nations—that of a duality, a pairing and/or balancing of opposite forces (the idea that male and female principles make a complete whole). The Igbo of eastern Nigeria express this concept in the adage, "where one thing stands, something else will stand beside it." It is this duality, this complementarity, this balance, that is symbolically expressed in most facets of African religions, culture, and sociopolitical organization. And the most powerful of these spiritual forces is the genderless African Great God—the highest-ranking monarch of the African spiritual political constituency.

Great God's Helpers: Goddesses

Great God's helpers are the lesser gods and goddesses. They are personifications of natural phenomena. They are powerful and worshipped. The Egyptian goddess *hathor* is a prehistoric goddess from whom all other gods and goddesses derived. Usually depicted as a woman with the head and ears of a cow, she personified the principles of joy, feminine love, and motherhood.[25]

Figure 1.1. Narmer Palette, Egypt, ca. 3100 BCE—Royal Ontario Museum. Photograph by Daderot, 20 November 2011.

The Egyptian goddess *nut* is the goddess of the sky. She regulates the times of the day by swallowing the sun in the evening and giving birth to it in the morning. Nut is hathor's sister and is wife to *geb*, the Egyptian god of the earth. With geb, nut gave birth to the gods and goddess *osiris, horus, seth,* and *isis.* Nut belongs to the first family of the deities in Egypt.[26] Nut's daughter, isis, is a goddess of healing. Her Pylon Temple was a great center of healing.[27] Another Egyptian goddess, *qadesh* (the holy one), is the goddess of love, sensuality, and fertility. She is most commonly depicted riding on the back of a lion, sometimes standing up, holding snakes, lotus buds, or papyrus plants—all symbols of fertility. Egyptians also worshipped qadesh as the goddess of nature.[28]

In Nubian country, *buk* is the river goddess of the Nuer of Sudan. She is believed to be the daughter of fireflies and guardian against crocodile attacks. Her presence is invoked by the sacrifice of a goat. Among the Dinka of the Sudan, buk is known as *abuk* or *acol.* Abuk or acol is a patron goddess of Dinka women as well as gardens. Her emblems are a small snake, the moon, and sheep.[29]

In the western part of the continent, the Yoruba of southwestern Nigeria worship a river and fertility goddess called *oshun.* She lives in a shrine in Oshogbo, Yorubaland, under which the Oshun River runs.[30] Oshun controls the Oshun River, which gives fertility to barren women who bathe in its water and pray to her. The goddess is celebrated annually in a nine-day festival.[31] In neighboring Benin, among the Fon, the goddess most closely identified with motherhood and childbearing is *minona* or *fa.* She exists in a paradoxical space: on the one hand, she is constructed as a goddess of mothering, birth, and nurturance; on the other hand, she is constructed as a goddess of witchcraft and death.[32] In her latter role, she is the patron goddess of witches, to whom she gives power.[33]

Among the Baga people of Guinea, *nimba* is the goddess of fertility, mother of the earth, and protector of pregnant women. She is the most important deity of the Baga.[34] Nimba is represented by a mask, which is also called *d'mba*.[35] She is powerful and beautiful and presides over all agricultural ceremonies. Nimba represents the joy of living. She is the promise of an abundant harvest. Nimba's presence is exemplified in all aspects of Baga life. She is present at weddings and showers and blesses new unions. She is present at harvest time to celebrate the fertility of crops. She is also present at funerals to usher the dead into the world of the ancestors.[36]

On the southern tip of the continent reigns *mbaba mwana waresa,* a Zulu goddess of the harvest, rain, and agriculture. She governs storm clouds, lightning, and thunder. The Zulus attribute the invention of beer to her. She also reigns over rainbows, which are a symbol of the connection between heaven and earth. The Zulu call on mbaba mwana waresa when they want guidance in making important decisions.[37] South Africa's neighbor, Zimbabwe, has a goddess called *dzivaguru.* She is the earth goddess of the Korekore people. A powerful deity who ruled both heaven and earth, she is the oldest of all Korekore deities, and the goddess of great wealth and medicinal power. She is depicted wearing goatskins and bearing many medicinal substances. Her sacred creatures are golden sunbirds.[38]

All these African goddesses, to varying degrees, served centrally important leadership roles in their societies. Their counsel was sought in everyday life, and they acted to enforce morality and build cooperation among societal groups. Most goddesses were highly complex and influential forces with particular functions, like protection and fertility, and met the needs of the peoples who worshiped them. As supernatural and authoritative forces, these goddesses influenced human life and reflected the values and traditions of their societies. They manifested their supernatural power to provide meaning, order, and ethics. In short, they were influential and authoritative leaders in the African spiritual political constituency.

Great God's Helpers: Oracles

Oracles are forces that predict the future and explain the past. They also, through their priests and priestesses, adjudicate and settle cases, and take care of other societal needs. In Arochukwu, eastern Nigeria, existed an all-powerful female oracle called *ibiniukpabi* (in Ibibio, "Drum of the Creator God"). She was known to the British as the Long Juju. The oracle originally belonged to the Ibibio and Efik peoples of the neighboring region. However, in the sixteenth century, the Aro seized control of the oracle, transforming it into a dreaded and powerful institution, whose power, authority, and influence were felt all over Igboland and beyond.

One of the reasons for ibiniukpabi's success was the fact that the new Aro custodians of the oracle were careful not to pit ibiniukpabi against the most powerful of all Igbo deities, *ani*, the earth goddess and creator of law or *omenani* (that which the goddess ani decrees to be right or wrong). Being a female oracle, ibiniukpabi's mouthpieces were men, who served her ably as priests. Ibiniukpabi served as the supreme court of the Aro people. She heard and settled cases, particularly murder, witchcraft, poisoning, and family cases. Her pronouncements were final. Offenders received their judgment by walking into ibiniukpabi's tunnel, otherwise known as the "tunnel of disappearance." If the accused was guilty, he or she would never be seen again. The offender would be "eaten up" by the "Red River," which would turn red as an indication to the offender's family that the said offender had been found guilty and ibiniukpabi had "eaten" him or her.

However, ibiniukpabi's priests became corrupted during the height of the transatlantic slave trade, and would, instead of carrying out her decrees, clandestinely redirect offenders to be carried away into slave networks.[39]

Great God's Helpers: Female Medicines

Medicines can be private or public, protective or aggressive. They can also be manipulated by the diviners

51

and priests who prepare them for the community. Some medicines are believed to derive their power from God. They are also believed to be able to act from a distance without direct contact. These medicines range from personal amulets or crossroad medicines to great, powerful shrine-type medicines that enjoy widespread high reputation.

The abolition of the transatlantic slave trade had a transformative effect on indigenous societies of western Africa. In fact, internal "slavery" continued unabated for many years, thus shepherding in a period of great instability in the West African interior. Even after the so-called destruction of ibiniukpabi between November 1901 and March 1903, Aro slave activity soared in the Igbo interior, wreaking incalculable havoc and destruction on the communities the Aro confronted.

In the mid- to late nineteenth century in the northern Igbo town of Alor-Uno, a great medicine, *adoro*, emerged in response to the incessant slave-raiding activities of the Aro and Nike. The people of Alor-Uno desired protection, a worthy protector from their neighbors' slave raiding. Thus, the community pooled its resources and engaged the services of the most powerful medicine-making family in the region. The medicine makers concocted a powerful protective *female* medicine called *adoro,* meaning *ka fa donata* (may they return), to both safeguard Alor-Uno's citizens from further devastation and appeal to the exiled Alor-Uno populace "to return home." And protect them she did. With adoro in place, no longer were the people of Alor-Uno cowed by the action of their enemy slavers. The Alor-Uno people were therefore able to remain in their present place.

In the course of her life, Alor-Uno people would elevate adoro from a medicine, which was merely venerated, to a universally respected and worshipped female deity who married wives in a process called *igo mma ogo* (becoming the in-law of a deity), therefore fulfilling the "birthing" responsibilities of the mother goddess. In fact, adoro remains one of the most powerful expressions of female religious and political power in Igboland. She is believed to be so powerful that as many as five male *attamas* (priests) are needed to minister to her, one in each of the Alor-Uno villages. The most senior attama serves as the *onyishi* (head) of all the attamas.[40]

Female Spiritual Monarchs: The Lovedu Rain Queens

Droughts are common in southern Africa and are a threat to the well-being of the nations of the region. Thus, Sotho-speaking people routinely practice rain rituals that are directed to the ancestors of their past rulers, asking that they intercede on their behalf. The Lovedu believe that if these rain rituals are not performed drought will occur.

Rain is essential for survival in the arid area the Lovedu inhabit. It is necessary for drinking water and subsistence farming. The Lovedu rain queen (*modjadji*) is the only one endowed with the power and authority to perform rituals and evoke the necessary medicine to bring forth rain. Rain queens also have the power to control and transform clouds into rain. They are therefore referred to as *khifidola-maru-a-daja* (transformer of clouds). Their power and authority also allow them to send rainstorms and hurricanes; and withhold rain from Lovedu enemies.

The rainmaking ceremony is one of most important rituals of the Lovedu. The ceremony is held annually at the beginning of the rainy or wet season. Sacred cycad trees are used in the rainmaking rites. The purpose of the rainmaking ritual is to appeal to the ancestors, gods, and goddesses to supply sufficient rain for human consumption and to ensure a good harvest and adequate grazing for livestock.

When rain is needed, the Lovedu sacrifice gifts to inform their rain queen of the "crying of her people" and the need for her to protect them. The rain queen then gathers secrets from her "rain potion" medicines, which are stored in rock shelters and prepared in clay pots. The chief ingredient used for rainmaking is the skin of a deceased chief. The rain queen grinds various medicines, empties them into a pot filled with water, and stirs so vigorously that froth appears on top of the pot. Once this happens, the pot will "create" rain. She also mixes medicine into the "rain horns," and when burnt, the smoke rises into the air and produces clouds. As the only being that can produce clouds, make and withhold rain, and make and withhold hurricanes, her power, authority, and influence are boundless.

In the Lovedu kingdom, the modjadji reigns supreme. Unlike elsewhere in Africa where there is a dual-sex or complementary system (in which male rulers take care of what is important to their male subjects, and female rulers take care of what is important to their female subjects), the Lovedu have exclusively female leadership structures. But this was not always so. Oral tradition suggests that the first rulers of the Lovedu were male. The first of these male rulers was one Makaphimo, who ruled the Lovedu until around 1800. Makaphimo was succeeded by his son Muhale. The Lovedu also had other male rulers, including Peduli, Khiali, and Mugede. The last known male leader was Mugede. During Mugede's reign, his rainmaking ability was in decline, and in order to rejuvenate these powers, Mugede committed incest with his daughter. This abominable act ushered in a shift in leadership from men to women. In fact, Mugede's daughter would become the first modjadji of the Lovedu.

Referred to by European observers and surrounding Africans as "She-Who-Must-Be-Obeyed," the modjadji was renowned, respected, and feared throughout Southern Africa. Lovedu kinship, politics, economy, and religion were united in the person of the rain queen. The modjadji was the living embodiment of the rain goddess; as such, she was inaccessible and mysterious. No one could claim to have seen the rain queen. This inaccessibility, compounded by the fact that the rain queen was immortal and thus could neither be killed nor die from natural causes, elevated the influence and authority that she had. In fact, the modjadji had to take her own life in ritual suicide—a selfless and powerful act—but not before she chose a successor.

Although the rain queen guaranteed the yearly seasonal cycle and fertility of crops, her emotions were believed to influence rain. If she was dissatisfied, angry, or sad she would not work well and the rain would not come. In 1934 or 1935, during the reign of Modjadji III, the first rains did not come until December. The consequential drought was attributed to her being upset about her daughter's liaison with a commoner.

There have been six rain queens in recent times: Maselekwane Modjadji I (1800–1854); Masalanabo Modjadji II (1854–95); Khesetoane Modjadji III (1896–1959); Makoma Modjadji IV (1959–80); Mokope Modjadji V (1981–2001); and Makobo Constance Modjadji VI (2003–5).

Maselekwane Modjadji I was feared for her power and famed for her diplomacy and influence. When she assumed office, she turned the chaos of her male predecessor's reign into peace and prosperity. She was, however, surrounded by restrictions that drove her into seclusion. She used Lovedu women for diplomacy by pacifying intruders in the Lovedu kingdom with beer and girls. She won fame and influence, which drew many foreign ambassadors to her court. Some came with cattle; others, with their daughters or sisters—gifts with which they would show homage or supplicate for rain. Some rain queens from far-away lands came to be strengthened and fitted for their office by the powerful modjadji. Even the Zulu king, Chaka, supplicated the Lovedu rain queen as "rain-maker of all rain-makers."[41] She governed without an official husband but was *female* husband to as many as forty-two wives, who did for their husband, the rain queen, what ordinary Lovedu women did for theirs, including hoeing her fields, brewing her beer, cooking her food, keeping her in domestic comfort, and trading for her. In 1854 Maselekwane committed ritual suicide.

Masalanabo Modjadji II succeeded her mother. Like her mother, she never married the father of her children but was a *female* husband who was cared for by her wives. As rain queen she was inaccessible to her people, and seldom appeared in public, further elevating her mystique and influence in society. Like her mother, she committed ritual suicide after having designated the daughter of her sister as her heir.

More than a century later, Makobo Constance would reign as modjadji. She was consecrated sixth rain queen of the Lovedu, on April 16, 2003, after the death of her grandmother. She was twenty-five years old. Her mother had been designated successor but died two days before her grandmother, Modjadji V. The youngest rain queen in the history of the Lovedu, the reluctant modjadji Makobo was the only rain queen who had been formally educated. On the day of her coronation, there was a slight drizzle, which was interpreted as a good omen. Makobo Constance, although respected for her power, abilities, and lineage, was seen as too modern to be a rain queen. Custom, for instance, dictated that rain queens live reclusive lives, hidden in the royal *kraal* with their wives. Makobo, however, wore jeans and T-shirts, visited dance clubs, watched soap operas, and chatted on her cell phone. She also had a boyfriend, David Mogale, a former municipal manager of the Greater Letaba Municipality. He was rumored to have moved into the Royal Compound, causing great controversy with the Royal Council, because the rain queen was only supposed to have sex with nobles the Royal Council chose. Thus, her lover was banned from the village, and the rain queen's two children were never recognized by the Council. On June 10, 2005, Makobo was admitted to Polokwane Medi-Clinic. She died two days later at the age of twenty-seven. The official cause of death was chronic meningitis.

For many years after Makobo died, no rain queen was named. Moreover, speculation was rife that because the rain queen's daughter was fathered by a commoner, the Lovedu were not likely to accept her as the rightful heiress to the rain queen crown. Therefore, there were worries that the 400-year-old powerful rain queen dynasty may have come to an end. These worries, however, abated in 2016, when eleven-year-old Masalanabo, daughter of Makobo, was recognized as Modjadji VII by President Jacob Zuma following the recommendations of South Africa's Commission on Traditional Leadership Disputes and Claims, also known as the Tolo Commission.[42]

Spirit Mediums: Human Interpreters of the Spiritual World

In the Nyamwezi areas of East Africa (present-day southern and western Uganda, Rwanda, Burundi, and northwestern Tanzania), women, in the 1800s, had an unusual degree of power, authority, and influence as spirit mediums which provided them with long-term, high-status positions. In the kingdoms of Bunyoro and Buganda (modern Uganda), Buha, Unyamwezi, and Usukuma (northwestern Tanzania), spirit possession societies centered on groups of legendary heroes known as the Cwezi or Imandwa. Cwezi were the early rulers of western Uganda. As the Cwezi kingdom declined, the people began to honor the spirits of their departed kings. In Rwanda and Burundi, the societies were dominated by spirits of their legendary heroes, Ryangombe and Kiranga. These possession societies were inclusive in their gender makeup.

Most Nyamwezi people lived in scattered settlements, spoke closely related Bantu languages, and were patrilineal. Their economic life revolved around combinations of agriculture and cattle raising. With the exception of the Kiga of southwestern Uganda, the Nyamwezi groups had centralized political structures. Bunganda, Bunyoro, Nkore, Rwanda, and Burundi were large relatively unified kingdoms whereas Buhaya, Buha, Unyamwezi, Usukuma, and Usumbwa were small states. All were hierarchical.

Few upper-class women were able to attain considerable wealth and authority. Spirit mediumship societies, therefore, provided women with the greatest avenues for active participation in politics and religious life. Spirit mediumship was a form of possession in which a person serves as intermediary between the spirits and society. Society interprets possession as a sign that a spirit or deity has chosen to inhabit a person for the good of the community. Spirit mediumship acknowledges communication between the supernatural world and the societal group the medium inhabits.

Spirit mediums were consulted either when difficulties arose or as a precautionary measure to ensure health, prosperity, and fertility. The people believed that if properly conciliated, their gods would, through spirit mediums, intercede on their behalf. Spirit mediums were able to accomplish this through either formal initiation or direct possession.

Spirit mediumship allowed women to transform into a higher sociopolitical and economic status. Spirit mediums were elevated and separated from regular society by the special regalia that they wore. They had secret vocabulary, possessed esoteric knowledge, and observed food taboos similar to those of upper classes. All spirit mediums viewed noninitiates as minors who were incapable of full participation in community affairs. Most important, spirit mediums possessed legal immunity.

Spirit mediums operated on different sociopolitical levels, concerning themselves with female activities such as fertility and agriculture. Spirit mediums had control and authority over their husbands during possession. Among the Soga of eastern Uganda, for instance, women ordered husbands to get rid of a concubine during possession. Mediums were powerful, authoritative, and respected. Mediumship gave women authority and license as well as access to substantial income. For example, in Bunyoro, a typical initiation ceremony song is: "You get plenty to eat and as well as that you put your hands in other people's purses." Moreover, spirit mediumship offered women a share of the influence and prerogatives of men. In Busoga, for instance, women could not ordinarily sit on stools. While possessed, however, they had their own skin seats and were treated as men. During Rundi ceremonies, women wore men's ceremonial dress, sat on stools, carried spears, and had the right to judge trials. In Rwanda, the *kubandwa* ceremony abolished sexual differences. All initiates, men and women, acquired the virile masculine quality called *umugabo*. Finally, spirit mediumship afforded women the power to express hostility against the social order or particular people. Possessed women had complete power and authority to express whatever feelings they had and take whatever actions they wished. This is because society accepted their words and actions as coming from a spirit. In Buha, initiates into spirit medium societies dress as their spirit and proclaim that they are no longer human beings but spirits.[43]

South of the Nyamwezi, impressive stone walls were constructed in present-day Zimbabwe by the ancestors of Shona people, the Karanga. These people, led by their Prince Mutota, formed the Mutapa or Monomotapa Empire, which derived wealth from large-scale gold mining. At its height in the fifteenth century, Great Zimbabwe's influence stretched from Zambezi River to the Kalahari, to the Indian Ocean, to the Limpopo River.

The Shona, like the Nyamwezi, venerate their ancestors and believe in spirit possession. In Mutapa, this ancestor veneration and spirit possession was elevated to astounding heights and influence with the establishment of royal *mhondoro* (lion) societies. Prince Mutota's son, Matope, announced that his spirit was immortal, and upon his death would enter a mhondoro, which in turn would wander the forests until it found a suitable medium.

Each mhondoro had its own "spirit province" that extended over one or more paramountcies. These mhondoros oversaw the well-being of entire regions. They were extremely powerful and influential. Their authority extended to advising nations, ensuring peace, and presiding over rainmaking, as well as other important ceremonies and rituals. Matope's sister Nyamhika Nehanda I, who possessed supernatural powers, also became a guardian royal mhondoro spirit.

In 1890, Cecil John Rhodes began his conquest of the area in the name of the British South African Company. He was most interested in exploiting the diamond and gold riches of the region. He started De Beers Consolidated Mines, Ltd., in 1888. By 1891, Rhodes co-owned 90 percent of the world's diamond mines. This British penetration and settlement led to the destruction of the political, economic, and religious order of the southern African people. The British also imposed a Hut Tax and forced labor, suppressed religious practices, and alienated African land. All this fueled the anger of the southern Africans who owned the land, and as a consequence, they were moved to resist.

The *chimurenga* military campaign, or "war of liberation," to drive out the British was started in May 1896 by the Ndebeles. The Shona joined them in October of the same year. A unique element of the chimurenga was the leading and authoritative roles played by three mhondoros—Mukwati in Matabeleland, Kagubi in western Mashonaland, and the female Nehanda II in central and northern Mashonaland. The mhondoros struck directly at the core of Shona beliefs, convincing them that Mwari, the Great God, blamed the whites for all their suffering and decreed that the whites should be driven from their land.

Nehanda II (ca. 1862–1898) was considered a female incarnation of the oracle spirit, Mbuya (grandmother) Nyamhika Nehanda, the grandmother of present-day Zimbabwe. Propelled by the instruction of Mwari, she rallied the Shona to intensify their struggle to expel the British. Using secret messages to communicate, all three mhondoros effectively coordinated their efforts. Kagubi was captured in October 1897, but Nehanda II eluded the British until December 1897. Both were summarily sentenced to death by hanging—Kagubi for the death of an African policeman, and Nehanda II for the death of Native Commissioner Pollard.

Kagubi subsequently converted to Christianity, but Nehanda II steadfastly refused, and went to her death in defiance, denouncing the British. Nehanda II's dying words, "My bones will rise again," predicted the second chimurenga, which culminated in the independence of present-day Zimbabwe. Despite British acts of horror and brutality against the people, as well as the fact that they faced superior technology, the chimurenga lasted until the end of 1897. British casualties, although numerically less, represented one-tenth of the settler population.

The people of present-day Zimbabwe still practice ancestor veneration and spirit possession. And between 1964 and 1979, Nehanda II's bones *did* rise again, this time in the person of an elderly female medium whose prophecies provided valuable intelligence for the war of independence. She would, however, not see independence, for she died in 1973. In a desperate attempt to diminish popular support for the Zimbabwe African National Liberation Army (ZANLA) during the second chimurenga, the then prime minister of Rhodesia (now Zimbabwe), Ian Smith, shamefully beseeched the names of the royal mhondoro. Today, Mbuya Nehanda, revolutionary prophet and leader of the first chimurenga in 1896, is now rightfully buried in Zimbabwe's Heroes' Acre.[44]

Figure 1.2. Nehanda Nyakasikana (*on left*) with Sekuru Kaguvi, following their capture. R. K. Rasmussen and Caroline du Sud Rupert, *Dictionnaire historique du Zimbabwe* (Scarecrow Press, 1990).

Diviners and Healers:
Human Interpreters of the Spiritual World

African healers diagnose illnesses. They prescribe and perform rituals intended to heal physical, mental, emotional, or spiritual ailments. In South Africa, the most highly respected of these healers is the sangoma. The sangoma, through divination, the prescription of herbal medicine, and the performance of rituals tailored for specific requirements, is able to cure ailments and restore well-being.

The Zulu believe that it is not uncommon for their ancestors, *amadlozi,* to meddle in the day-to-day life of human beings. Their meddling can take the form of sending illness (*isifo*) to the living. They do so not because they are wicked, but to punish the living for violations of the ethical standards for communal living, including failing to conduct important rituals or violating taboos. The ancestors' wrath can manifest itself in illness visited upon the offending individuals. Individuals thus afflicted are considered spiritually polluted and imbalanced and must be restored. This is where the sangoma comes in. She has the power and know-how to determine the cause of the ailment, that is, whether it is physical or spiritual, and then determine the rituals that must be conducted in order to appease the offended ancestors and restore the person to good health.

Sangomas also search out illness caused by witches and sorcerers. Witchcraft is dreaded because it can cause devastation to a person's life. For this reason, individuals often take precautionary measures to circumvent this evil. The sangoma has the power and authority to perform rituals to neutralize these malevolent forces and appeal to the ancestors for protection against the witches and sorcerers. She also has the power and knowledge to create protective amulets and to channel fragrances from medicinal plants to effect spiritual cleansing.

Sangomas are respected because of their super-natural power and the influence they have in society. A sangoma summons this power (*umbilini*) at will through beating a drum or deep meditation. She is also able to access the knowledge of the world—past and present—to influence the future.[45]

Priestess-Healers, Priestesses, Prophetesses, and Male Priestesses of Goddesses

Priestesses of deities serve as the mediums through which the spirits and deities communicate their power-ful messages to the human world and operate. As early as 23 BCE, during the Kushite rule over Egypt, the position of chief priestess (*dewat neter*) of the god *amun* was held by the daughter of the Meroitic (present-day Sudan) king, and this position gave her great economic and political influence. Even after the Kushite loss of Egypt, Meroitic royal women continued to hold important po-sitions and wield considerable power in the temples of amun at Napata (ancient Nubia) and elsewhere.[46]

Among the Ghanaian Asante, during important cultural festivities like the Adae kɛdeɛ, or the great Adae festival, many priestesses become possessed and voice the messages of the deities, gods, or goddesses. Likewise, during the funeral ceremonies of great kings and queen mothers such as the Asantehene or Asantehemma, priestesses are seen doing the same. In everyday life, priestesses are visited by clients who desire a connection with a given deity.[47]

The *basangu* prophetesses of the Tonga of Zambia are the custodians of the *basangu* deity, who represents ordered society. Basangu prophetesses have the power and authority to withhold rain and send epidemics or other trouble to alert communities to their demands. They also do this as a punishment for disrespecting them and their chosen sites.[48]

In the West African city of Whydah, Benin, the people venerate snakes, especially the nonpoisonous python. Female servants serve these python deity-spirits as mediums, who while in trance relay messages from the python gods, whereas *male* priestesses called snake wives (*dangbe-si*) see to the day-to-day needs of the

Figure 1.3. Temple of the Pythons, Ouidah, Benin. Photograph by Dan Sloan, March 19, 2017.

python deity or spirit, including feeding the python deities. These Beninese, as well as the Igbos, Ijaws, and Ibibios of the Nigerian Niger Delta, show extreme reverence to pythons; they are not allowed to kill them, and if they find a dead python, they bury it in a white cloth like a human being. Thus, the female mediums of these deity pythons are powerful and influential because they communicate the authority of their deity python.[49]

In present-day Ghana, Nana Afua Nsiah, a priestess-healer, lives in a small village, Nsiakrom, fifty miles away from Kumasi. When a spirit begins to show itself in her, a dramatic physical transformation takes place, and depending on what spirit possesses her, the priestess-healer evokes the manner and style of the possessing spirit. Sometimes Nana Afua Nsiah becomes a warrior, a royal personage, or even a Christian pastor, demonstrating that the African religious pantheon is flexible and fluid enough to evolve new deities, including Christian "deities." When possessed of the various spirits, Nsiah exudes the power, authority, and influence of her deity. She gives advice, prescribes medicine, and helps recover lost items. She also serves the important function of diagnosing severe illnesses such as mental illness, leprosy, blindness, barrenness, and impotence. Beyond this, she helps determine the reason for poor harvests, trade, and other economic enterprises.[50] It is the authority that Nsiah has as a result of her connection to the spirit world that positions her as an influential, respected leader her villagers find necessary to consult.

In the Senegambia region, the Diola prophetess, Ali-nesitoué Diatta, otherwise known as one of the women of Emitai, communicated directly with Emitai. She was a revolutionary who had tremendous influence on Diola society. Subsuming the power and authority of Emitai, she was a sociopolitical force who knew that colonialism and the Second World War had amplified local Diola crises such as the drought. She therefore channeled her power into creating and introducing new shrine houses that would address new community problems, address persistent problems more effectively and efficiently, and spread access to Emitai's supernatural power.[51] Diatta thus became the medium through which the powerful and authoritative teachings of the Great God, Emitai, were disseminated.

In this chapter, I have explored the political working of female entities in the spiritual world; starting with the most powerful genderless African Great God—the ultimate leader of the spiritual political constituency, whose power, though appearing distant, is felt by all— and touching on the power and authority of African goddesses, spirit mediums, priestesses (both male and female), prophetesses, diviners, and healers. Each serves a central, powerful and influential, supernatural role in the governance of their societies.

Chapter 2 documents women's power, authority, and influence in the human political constituency through representative case studies from east to south, north to west Africa.

2

Queens, Queen Mothers, Princesses, and Daughters

The African women who have occupied the uppermost leadership positions in their societies have achieved that status in various ways. They have rarely served alone as supreme sovereigns:[1] they have shared joint sovereignty in a system of complementary rule with their male counterparts. The criteria by which they succeed to office, the meaning of their titles, and the functions they perform vary from one locality to the next. What these women have in common is that each has occupied a position equal or complementary to that of the monarch, and that they have often performed functions derived from the mothering and protecting potential inherent in womanhood.[2] A queen, queen mother, or princess typically assumes her position by virtue of birth, heredity, and (less frequently) marriage. She could be the king's biological mother; a classificatory[3] mother, sister, daughter, relative, in-law, or wife; or appointed in her own right. The offices are politically significant, and these women leaders exert considerable influence over men's offices.

This chapter focuses on the human political constituency, documenting the lives and times of a representative sample of queens, queen mothers, princesses, and daughters from different times and parts of Africa, including queens Nefertiti of Egypt and Amina of Hausaland; queen mothers Yaa Asantewa of Ejisu, Asanteland, Iyoba Idia of the Kingdom of Benin, and Labotsibeni Mdluli of Eswatini; princesses Inikpi of the Igala Kingdom and Magogo of Zululand; and the *omus* of Igboland, Nigeria. It centers their lives of influence while posing the questions: To whom were these women accountable? On whose behalf did they exercise power?

The Female Principle in African Politics: The Human Political Constituency

The human political constituency is a dual-sex system in which women assume leadership roles in a fashion complementary to male rulers. In centralized African systems, women rule variously as queens, queen mothers, empresses, and princesses; in small or egalitarian societies, groups of elderly women rule as daughters. A case study of Egyptian women rulers captures the essence of this complementary system but also complicates the accepted narrative by bearing witness to women who ruled as queen regents in place of young male pharaohs or as wives of pharaohs (this chapter) and in their own right as *female* pharaohs (see chapter 4).

Queens and Queen of the Ladies

Queen Ahhotep was the queen regent of Egypt during the late Seventeenth Dynasty (ca. 1560–1530 BCE). She ruled on behalf of young Pharaoh Kamose, who might have been her brother-in-law or son. After her husband fell in battle, she is said to have continued the struggle against the Hyksos, whose invasion, occupation, and subsequent rule of Egypt had led to the end of the Thirteenth Dynasty and ushered in the Second Intermediate Period. An Eighteenth Dynasty inscription remembers her in this way: "She assembled her fugitives. She brought together her deserters. She pacified her Upper Egyptians. She subdued her rebels."[4]

Then there was Nefertiti, known for her incredible beauty (her name translates as "a beautiful woman has come"), the great royal wife or chief consort of Pharaoh Akhenaten of the New Kingdom. By the end of her husband's reign (ca. 1353–1336 BCE), and with a push from the royal couple, *aten* (or *aton*), the sun god, had become Egypt's dominant national god. She therefore changed her name to Neferneferuaten-Nefertiti, which means "beautiful are the beauties of aten, a beautiful woman has come," to symbolize her recognition of aten (or aton) as Egypt's national god. Nefertiti and Akhenaten were connoisseurs of Egyptian art, which they unfailingly encouraged.

Very little physical evidence has survived about Queen Twosret, who was wife of Seti II, queen regent,

Figure 2.1. Bust of Nefertiti, Queen Consort of Akhenaten, 18th
Dynasty, Egypt. Photograph by Philip Pikart, November 8, 2009.

then pharaoh, and the last known ruler of the Nineteenth Dynasty of Egypt. Her birth name, Twosret, means "mighty lady, chosen of Mut," and her royal name, Sitre Meryamun, means "daughter of Re, beloved of Amun." After Seti II died, his young son Ramesses-Siptah, by his third wife Tiaa, ascended to the throne of Egypt. Because Ramesses-Siptah was in his teens, Twosret assumed the role of queen regent. Siptah died six years later, making way for Twosret to formally ascend to the throne of Egypt herself between 1187 and 1185 BCE.

Meroë, in present-day Sudan, which has been described as Africa's second great civilization, had so many women leaders that the outside world believed that it never had a king.[5] It became the southern administrative center of the kingdom of Cush or Kush around 750 BCE. Meroë royal women, referred to as *kandake,* transliterated as candace, held prominent positions in the political running of their kingdoms, wielding authority, influence, and power. *Kandake* means "great woman," and derives from the Meroitic title *kdke,* ascribed to all royal consorts, including kings' wives, queen mothers, and ruling queens. Although little historical evidence about these royal women has survived, it is believed that there were at least ten kandakes between 260 BCE and 320 CE, and no fewer than six between 60 BCE and 80 CE in Meroë.[6] One appears in Acts of the Apostles, 8:27, as Candace. Another kandake ruled in 61 BCE, and her rule was documented by the Roman emperor Nero.

The names of at least nine ruling kandakes of Kush at Meroë have survived, including Bartare (ca. 260–250 BCE), who was buried in one of the three pyramids in Meroë's south cemetery; Shanakhdakheto or Shanak-dakhete (ca. 177–155 BCE), the first known kandake to have ruled alone, and whose tomb was inscribed with the first known Meroitic hieroglyphs; Amanirenas (ca. 40–10 BCE), who might have ruled jointly with her husband, Prince Akinidad, and reigned during a period of great prosperity (two surviving portraits from her pyramid lend clues to her rule: in the first, she is dressed in ceremonial clothes and is spearing bound prisoners; the second portrait shows the presence of three scars under her left eye, supporting the hypothesis that she might in fact be the one-eyed kandake who fought the Romans during the 20s BCE); Amanishakheto (ca. 10 BCE–1 CE), who is mentioned in several monuments and whose collection of jewelry was discovered in her pyramid; Amanirenas (ca. 1–20 CE), who ruled jointly with her husband, King Natakamani, and is remem-bered with him as the greatest builders of the Meroitic kingdom, who restored the temples of Amon in Na-pata and Meroë; Amantitere (ca. 20–49 CE), probably the kandake identified in Acts 8:27, whose treasury was managed by the Ethiopian Eunuch; Amanikha-tashan (ca. 62–85 CE), who ruled the kingdom after the golden age of Meroë, a peaceful time, during which the kingdom made connections with India and began to worship the Asian god *apedemek,* a lion deity with three

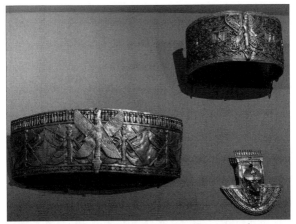

Figure 2.2. Jewelry of Amanishakheto from her pyramid at Meroe. Photograph by Einsamer Schütze, September 22, 2006.

heads and several arms; Maleqorobar (ca. 266–283 CE); and Lahideamani (306–314 CE). No other kandakes are remembered by name after Lahideamani's death. There might, however, have been a kandake who ruled around 317 CE and died in 326 CE, at which time the Kingdom of Meroë would have almost completely disappeared.[7]

In the Horn of Africa, a chronicle of Ethiopian dynastic succession from Menelik I (957 BCE) includes six queens or kandakes. Nicauta Kandake (730–681 BCE), was the first kandake; and after her there were at least five regnant kandakes[8] who ruled between 332 BCE and 50 CE. The record chronicles twenty-one regnant kandakes—several of whom played important roles in Ethiopian history—ruling until the ninth century. Three kandakes central to Ethiopian dynastic history were Makeda, queen of Saba or Sheba, who founded the Menelik or Solomonic dynasty that exercised power until the 1974 overthrow of Haile Selassie; Queen Ahywa (or Sofya), who in 332 CE turned Christianity into the official religion of the kingdom; and Gudit, Yodit, Judith, or Esato (Fire), a kandake of Jewish origin, who invaded Aksum and overthrew its king. She would ultimately cause the downfall of the empire, and found the rival Zagwe dynasty (933–1253 CE). After Gudit, no other regnant queens appear in the record until the empress of Ethiopia, and daughter of Menelik II, Queen Zaudita, who ruled at the time of Abyssinia's offensive against Italian colonial invasion in the 1930s.[9]

In the present-day country of South Africa, Queen Manthatisi (1781–1836) became queen regent after her husband passed away in 1815. She did so on behalf of her young son, Sekonyela, who was still a child. For approximately a decade, Manthatisi fulfilled the duties of king: consulting with advisors, exercising political and military authority, and arbitrating disputes. Queen Manthatisi was a strong, brave, capable, but physically slight leader, whose followers affectionately called her *mosayane* (the tiny one). Manthatisi ruled during a time of great scarcity and famine. She led her people to raid cattle and grain from her neighbors. So great was her reputation that she evoked considerable terror in the hearts and minds of the inhabitants of the neighboring nations. Although she came from the nation of Batlokwa, during her reign her people came to be known as Manthatisi. Moreover, Queen Manthatisi was able to ward off the incessant raids of the Nguni people during the *mfecane/difaqane*[10] wars and keep her people together.[11]

In present-day Nigeria, the *iyalode* (queen of ladies), like male chiefs of Yorubaland, is a chief in her own right. She has her own special insignia of office, including a necklace of special beads, wide-brimmed straw hat, and shawl. She also has her own personal servants and special drummers and bell ringers who call the women of the kingdom to attention. Bearing the title *eiyelobinrin* (mother of all women), the iyalode has jurisdiction over all women. The iyalode's position is achieved, not inherited, and she is the chosen representative of all women. Hers is an elected office, which has to have the stamp of popular approval. The iyalode's most important qualifications are her proven ability to lead, her ability to articulate the feelings of the women, her control of vast economic resources, and her popularity.

Once appointed, the iyalode becomes not only the voice of women in government but also the queen who coordinates their activities. She settles quarrels in court and meets with women to determine what the women's stand should be on such questions as declarations of war, the opening of new markets, and the administration of women at local levels.

As spokesperson of the women, she is given access to all positions of power and authority within the state. She exercises legislative, judicial, and executive powers with male chiefs in their council. She has her own council of subordinate women chiefs who exercise jurisdiction over all women in matters that pertain to them, working to settle disputes between women and other women's concerns. The iyalode also controls all markets. In addition, she is the honorary president-general for all the women's societies in town. A great deal of what she can achieve depends on her qualities as iyalode: her personality, dynamism, ability to lead and influence, and political astuteness.[12]

Other Warrior Queens/Queen-Mothers

In addition to the Ethiopian Gudit, other African female leaders in the human political constituency were known for their warrior instincts, including Al-Kahina of the Maghreb; the Luena NyaKarolo of Angola, who during her reign instituted a system of female chiefdoms in all the countries she conquered; Queen Amina of Hausaland; and Queen Mother Yaa Asantewa of the Asante.

Remembered by the Berbers as the "Berber warrior queen" or "queen of the *aures*" (mountains), by the Arabs as "queen of Ifriqiya and the Maghrib," by the Jews as the "Berber Deborah," and by the French as the sponsor of the "last heroic resistance to the Arabs," Al-Kahina was known for her cunning and military prowess. She viciously defended her homeland during several battles including the 693–698 CE Arab invasion of the Maghreb, which led to her defeat and early death by execution.[13]

Queen Amina or Aminatu (fifteenth or sixteenth century) of Hausaland (present-day Nigeria) was a warrior woman and eldest daughter of Queen Turunku and was said to have created and ruled without interruption the great Hausa Empire from about 1536 to 1573 CE and to have expanded her empire's boundaries to the Atlantic coast. She did so by leading a fierce army of twenty thousand horsemen into battle, annexing surrounding states and demanding tributes from them. The ruins of some of her fortifications still stand today. Her reign saw the expansion and spread of kola nut cultivation and the establishment of long-distance trade routes into North Africa. Indeed, so powerful is the memory of her exploits that songs of her deeds are still sung today.[14]

The matrilineal Kom of the Cameroonian Bamenda grassfields are organized into *fondoms* (chiefdoms), which are ruled by *fons* (kings). Bamenda was the second-largest grassfield fondom after Nso. The Kom fondom was founded in the middle of the nineteenth century. According to Kom oral traditions, their ancestors migrated from Ndobo in northern Cameroon. These oral traditions relay an early history in which Kom women played a prominent role in defending their fondom from their neighbors, the Mejang, Ajung, Bafmeng, and Kijem. The women utilized and evolved the *anlu* ("to drive away"), an indigenous women's organization to seek redress for crimes committed against their nation. Kom oral tradition tells us about anlu's origins.

Long ago, the Kom were forced into being a vassal state under the neighboring fondoms of Ajung and Mejang, and this meant that Kom had to pay annual tribute in the form of labor for the construction of the Mejang palace with castor oil and mud. The Kom got tired of paying this tribute and refused to provide this labor. The Mejang interpreted this as an act of rebellion and planned a punitive expedition against the Kom when the Mejang believed the Kom men had gone on a hunting expedition. Their plan was to capture all Kom women and children to force the Kom to continue to provide labor for them. However, information about their plan leaked out to the queen mother of the Kom, or *Nafoyn*, through her network of female spies. The queen mother mobilized all Kom women, who were asked to disguise themselves as men by donning their husbands' attire and arming themselves with their husbands' weapons. Thus, when the Mejang men attacked, they were confronted by a formidable force of Kom "men," who were actually women in disguise. The Mejang men took off running. In the scuffle, several Mejang died, and some escaped. The Kom women were, however, able to capture one of the men. After the women stripped themselves of their warrior attire, their Mejang prisoner was bewildered to discover that the attacking force was an army of women. The Kom women beat him mercilessly and threatened his life. Then they sent him back with strict instructions to his king never to ask for any service or tribute from the Kom again. From that time on, the anlu came to be recognized as a powerful and reputable organization for handling state affairs. It is, in essence, a disciplinary organization, with a military for defending the rights of women and the state. Thus, whenever the interests of Kom women are affected, the anlu is expected to step in forcefully.[15]

The British found few people as difficult to subdue as the Asante of what is now Ghana. The Asante wars against the British, which began in 1805, lasted 100 years. Although outmatched by superior weaponry, the Asante kept the British army at bay for a short final period of independence. To understand the Asante wars, one must look at the roles of a few of Asante's warrior rulers. First, Queen Mother Yaa Akyaa, who came to power in 1884 after destooling her mother (see the next section for the meaning of the queen mother's stool), who was queen mother during a time of intense upheaval resulting from the British encroachment on Asante sovereignty. An immensely rich and powerful ruler, Yaa Akyaa amassed firearms, waged war, engineered political campaigns and succession struggles, and ordered the execution of her brother and other rivals. She was strategic in her alliances. She married two brothers in turn who were members of the royal family and thus likely to support her in internal succession struggles. She further extended this political support by giving all seven of her daughters in marriage to important chiefs.[16]

In 1891, when Yaa Akyaa's son, King Prempeh I, was pressured to sign a protection treaty, he resolved not to submit to British control of Asante, instead telling the British envoy: "The suggestion that Asante in its present state should come and enjoy the protection of Her Majesty the Queen and Empress of India, is a matter of very serious consideration and I am happy to say we have arrived at this conclusion, that my kingdom of Asante will never commit itself to any such policy. Asante must remain [independent] of old."[17]

In 1897, the British exiled King Prempeh and informed the Asante that he would never return. King Prempeh and queen mother Yaa Akyaa lived out their days in British-imposed exile. Then in 1899, in a further attempt to humiliate the Asante, the British sent their governor, Sir Frederick Hodgson, to Kumasi to demand the Golden Stool (*sika dwa*), a symbol of Asante unity.

That evening, the Asante chiefs held a secret meeting in Kumasi to discuss how they could force the British to bring back their king. Yaa Asantewa, the queen mother of Ejisu, observed that some of the chiefs were cowed. In her now famous challenge, she declared:

> How can a proud and brave people like the Asante sit back and look while white men took away their king and chiefs and humiliate them with a demand for the Golden Stool. The Golden Stool only means money to the white man; they searched and dug everywhere for it. . . . Is it true that the bravery of the Asante is no more? I cannot believe it. . . . If you, the chiefs of Asante, are going to behave like cowards and not

fight, you should exchange your loincloths for my undergarments. . . . If you the men of Asante will not go forward, then we will. We the women will. I shall call upon my fellow women. We will fight the white men. We will fight till the last of us falls in the battlefields.[18]

That was the beginning of the Yaa Asantewa War. The final battle began on September 30, 1900, and ended in the bloody defeat of the Asante. Yaa Asantewa was last to be captured, and subsequently exiled to the Seychelles, where she died around 1921. With the end of these wars, Britain gained control of the hinterland of Ghana.

Queen Mothers and Reign Mates

Asante queen mothers are corulers and derive their power from the matrilineal nature of social organization. The Asante have a saying: "It is a woman who gave birth to a man, it is a woman who gave birth to a king." Queen mothers of Asanteland have their own stools, which symbolize power and authority, just as the European throne does for monarchies. The queen mother's stool epitomizes the fact that she holds office on the basis of her own qualifications, not those of a husband. Queen mothers determine succession and inheritance as well as the rights and obligations of citizens.

At the very top of the Asante Empire hierarchy is the *asantehemma* (female) and the *asantehene* (male). The Asante Empire is divided into paramounts, governed by the paramount queen mothers (*ahemaa*) and the paramount chiefs (*amanhene*). Ahemaa are the corulers who hold joint responsibility with the male chiefs in all matters of state. Under the paramounts are the towns, which are governed by their own queen mothers (called the *mma paninfuo*) and chiefs (*odikro*) of lesser status than the ahemaa and amanhene. The mma paninfuo occupy one of the two stools in the town, which serve jointly as visible symbols of political authority. Under the towns are eight clans, all of which are governed by queen mothers of the clans, called *mbusuapanyinfuo*.

The Asante queen mother exercises power, authority, and influence in many domains. She is in charge of female governance in the empire, paramounts, towns, and clans. But her most important duty concerns her responsibilities to the king. She selects the king. She is the royal genealogist who determines the legitimacy of all claimants to the king's vacant stool. When a king's stool becomes vacant, the queen mother nominates a candidate for the Golden Stool. She has three chances to nominate a suitable candidate, who must be approved by the traditional Asante council. In addition, the queen mother guides and advises the king on all matters of state, tradition, and religion. She performs important rituals for her people, such as the initiation rites for young women before they start menstruating, and is also present during important ceremonies like funerals. She ensures that taboos are not breached. Moreover, she is the only one who has the right to criticize and rebuke the king in public. As a member of the governing council or assembly of state, the queen mother's presence is required whenever important matters of state are to be decided. Each queen mother has her own separate court in her palace where she is assisted by female counselors and functionaries. She hears all judicial cases involving sacred oaths of the state and maintains independent jurisdiction over all domestic matters affecting women and members of the royal family. She can interfere in judicial proceedings heard by the king and grant pardons or modify sentences imposed by the king. Moreover, male litigants can apply to have their civil cases transferred from the king's court to the queen mother's court. If the queen mother agrees to hear the case, her judgment is binding. Finally, unlike most women, when married, the queen mother has the right to have affairs with men in the kingdom or empire.[19]

In the Fon kingdom of Dahomey in present-day Benin, the *kpojito* ("mother of the leopard") is the "reign mate" of the king. Between 1740 and 1774, Hwanjile ruled as high priest and kpojito. Hwanjile was an Aja trader and mother of two before being taken to the court of Abomey. Some accounts indicate that she was a captive from the village of Home near Abomey. In the mid-eighteenth century, the kingdom of Dahomey had set its expansionist sights on Hwanjile's home country of Aja, southwest of Dahomey. After conquering Aja country, King Tegbesu married Hwanjile, and then appointed her to the position of kpojito to help cement

Dahomey's control over this newly conquered land. She would become the richest, most powerful, and most influential woman in the kingdom. The new kpojito was supposed to act as an informant on her conquered homeland. Hwanjile helped Tebgesu consolidate his power by wiping out the local priests who supported some would-be usurpers of his throne. She ingeniously imported the two forces of the creation God, *Mawu* and *Lisa,* from her native Aja and established them as the rulers of the Dahomean religious pantheon, building a shrine for them outside her palace and serving as their high priestess. Several gods that are still worshipped by the Fon today are attributed to Hwanjile.[20]

In neighboring Nigeria, as the kingdom of Benin expanded, the *iyoba* (queen mother), Idia (1504-1550), rose to prominence by producing the *oba* or the king's first son, Esigie. She was rewarded for this by being elevated to the rank of a powerful male. Being the woman who had given birth to the next king, the queen mother rose in prominence over the king's other wives. She had an important state function. She acted on behalf of her son and contributed immensely to Benin's growth, as well as tying the kingdom together. The queen mother was attended by female slaves and eunuchs and shielded from her subjects. The only people who could communicate with her directly were members of the king's family and other royal wives.[21]

Popularly known as *Gwamile* or *Mgwami,* the greatest twentieth-century stateswoman of the tiny, landlocked country of Eswatini was the *ndlovukazi* or Queen Mother Labotsibeni Mdluli. Labotsibeni Mdluli was referred to as "the great she elephant," a term that captured her immense influence and power as well as her outstanding intellect and value in the kingdom. She was said to have been one of the shrewdest, most influential, and most astute regents to have ruled the Swazi from the death of Mbandeni in 1889 until 1921. In fact, the kingdom owes its existence today largely to Mdluli's determination and achievements. As the European invaders settled, they laid claim to Eswatini, undermining the political authority of the Swazi ruler and the sovereignty of the Swazi. It was against this backdrop that Labotsibeni became ndlovukazi. Her rule was an endless struggle for human rights and social justice for her people. In 1903, Labotsibeni led her people to protest successfully against the Order-in-Council that placed Eswatini under direct control of the Transvaal.[22]

In the kingdom of Buganda, in present-day Uganda, the queen mother or mother of the king had autonomous authority. She utilized this authority to check the king's excesses and protect the nation. Queen mothers were not just women rulers; they supported, advised, defended, protected, punished, and nurtured the king, and by extension, the nation. Ganda queen mothers were king makers. They mobilized their lineages and allies to support their sons in becoming the next kings.[23]

The queen mother's authority mirrored that of the king. Just as the king appointed his ministers, allocated land, and collected taxes, the queen mother appointed her own ministers (who mirrored those of the king) and had them collect taxes on land that she exclusively controlled. Moreover, the queen mother's prime minister, her second-in-command, and her appointed chiefs did not have to obey the king or his ministers. In 1862, for instance, when explorer John Hanning Speke visited the Ganda capital, the king forbade anyone to visit him. Speke, however, received a visit from Sabaganzi, the brother of Queen Mother Muganzirwaza, at her request. No other Ganda person dared break the king's pronouncement for fear of his retribution.

Because the queen mother owned a wealth of land in various parts of the kingdom, she had economic independence from the king. The Ganda people who lived on her land served her and not the king. Some of these subjects worked as fishermen for the queen mother. Moreover, the queen mother's land was exempt from taxation by the king.

The queen mother never visited the king, but the king visited her regularly at her court, where she received the same kinds of tributes that the king did. In the mid-nineteenth century, the leading and most powerful spirit mediums of the Cwezi lived with the queen mother. Thus, her palace became the center of spiritual power in the kingdom.[24]

Princesses and Warrior Princesses

African princesses rule because they are either daughters of a ruling monarch, a female relative of a monarch, the granddaughter of a monarch, or the wife or widow of a prince. The case studies that follow are examples of African warrior princesses and regular princesses, spread across regions and time.

Princess Kifunji (1623–1647), christened Grace, was the daughter of Kia Samba and Guenguela Cakombe and sister of Mukambu Barbara and Nzingha Anna Mbande. She was also an influential member of the Council of Government in the kingdoms of Matamba and Ndongo in present-day Angola and Congo. She and her sister Mukambu served as their sister King Nzingha's (see chapter 4) closest aides, advisors, and confidantes. Princesses Kifunji and Mukambu were military leaders. They wore matching animal-skin uniforms and fought in King Nzingha's army with an arsenal of swords, axes, bows, and arrows. Princess Kifunji was also an important religious leader. In October 1647, she was drowned by the invading Portuguese as their army retreated. Her sister Mukambu led an army that continued to fight the Portuguese into the late 1650s.[25]

Sometime during the last decade of the seventeenth century, in present-day northern Nigeria, the *aku* or Jukun king sent his emissaries to collect the annual tribute from the Igala kingdom. Ayegba, the *attah* or king of Igala, filled the aku's containers with stones and dung and sent his messengers back with a warning that the Igala people would no longer pay tribute to the Jukun. On receiving this news, the enraged aku declared war on Ayegba and the Igala.

Because the Jukun kingdom was the stronger kingdom, an Igala defeat seemed like a foregone conclusion. Attah-Ayegba, in an attempt to circumvent this defeat, consulted a seer who revealed that he would have to sacrifice his beloved daughter, Inikpi, to the gods if the Igala kingdom wished to win the war. A shaken Ayegba kept this chilling prophecy to himself and did nothing. Princess Inikpi grilled her father's closest confidants, and once she found out the seer's prophecy, her action was as brave as it was swift. She ordered that a large hole be dug near the bank of the Niger and Benue rivers. Then to the horror of her subjects, Princess Inikpi descended into the hole, accompanied by nine of her slaves, and she ordered that it be tightly closed with earth. Princess Inikpi had been buried alive.

Because of the courage and selflessness shown by young Princess Inikpi, her people elevated her to the rank of a goddess. She presently occupies the special space of chief intermediary between the Igala and their Great God, Ojo. A deified Inikpi has also been constructed as the protector of all Igalas—a merciful mother who safeguards and intercedes on behalf of her children in time of trouble. She is also considered a goddess of fertility who is believed to grant children to barren Igala women. Each year during the kingdom's most important festival, Ocho, the attah and his senior chiefs offer sacrifices at Princess Inikpi's shrine. Today her statue stands at the Idah open market, near the confluence of the Niger and Benue rivers, marking the

Figure 2.3. Statue of Princess Inikpi, Idah Market, Kogi State. Photograph by Nwando Achebe, Idah, Kogi State, Nigeria, July 2007.

spot where Inikpi gave her life for the victory of her people.[26]

She has been called a princess, a queen, and even a *female* king; but one fact remains indisputable, that Tassi Hangbè of Abomey, in the kingdom of Dahomey, in present-day Benin, ruled as sole monarch for a short time, roughly between 1708 and 1711. She ruled after the death of her twin brother Akaba, who was king and who had passed away after a short illness. She was said to have disguised herself as her brother and led her troops into the final battle of Lissèzoun, where they defeated the kingdom of Wémè. Back in Abomey, her nephew (Akaba's son) was too young to ascend the throne, so Hangbè took over and would become one of Dahomey's most important rulers, reigning until 1740.[27]

In the Zulu Kingdom of present-day South Africa, during the chieftaincy of Jama in the 1770s, his three daughters became heads and leaders of the *izigodlos* or military harems. Mkabayi headed the *ebaQulusini* or "where they pushed out buttocks" harem. Another daughter, Mmana, headed the *Osebeni* or "on the river-bank" harem, and his third daughter, Mawa, headed the *'seNtonteleni* or "in the bend of the river" harem. When Jama died in 1781, Princess Mkabayi (1750–1843) ruled as regent for her young brother, Senzangakhona. Mkabayi assumed the role of *impi,* or the spiritual leader of the Zulu army. She was believed to be strong, ruthless, and manipulative. She never married but maintained her independence, political influence, and power as the head of the AbaQulusi military palace. She was celebrated by both men and women and is remembered in praise songs that have lasted to the present day.[28]

Between 1831 and 1840, Regent Princess Menem Leben Amande of Yejje ruled in present-day Ethiopia. She commanded her own army and assumed the position of regent for her son Ras Ali Aula. In 1840, she married Yohannes II and became empress of Ethiopia. She became extremely powerful, so much so that two years later her husband Yohannes launched a rebellion against her. In 1847, she was wounded and captured in battle, but her son, Aula, ransomed her, and she ruled until 1853.

Mukaya was a warrior princess or *mwanana* of the Luba people, in present-day Congo-Brazzaville, in

Central Africa. In the late nineteenth century, she and her brother, Kasongo Kalambo, led their Luba people in battle against enemy nations in an attempt to shore up their family's claim to the throne. After her brother Kalambo was killed in battle, mwanana Mukaya assumed control of the Luba empire, which at the time stretched from the rain forest of present-day Zaire to northern Zambia.[29]

Born to Empress Menen and Emperor Haile Selassie of Ethiopia, Princess Tenagnework Haile Selassie (1912–2003) received her title after her father became emperor in November 1930. She became the most prominent woman in the Imperial Ethiopian court after her mother's death in 1961 and was among the emperor's closest advisers. A strong personality with conservative views, Princess Tenagnework was one of the few who could criticize official Ethiopian policy to the emperor. She was a staunch defender of the monarchy during an era of rapid change. When the emperor was deposed by a military coup in 1974, the imperial family was imprisoned for fifteen years. A year after their 1989 release, Princess Tenagnework went into exile, returning to Ethiopia in 1999. A mother of seven children, Princess Tenagnework was married three times. Her first husband was Ras Desta Damtew, governor of Sidamo Province. She then married Ato Abebe Retta, who served as ambassador in the postwar imperial government and would become president of the Imperial Senate after their separation. Her third spouse was Ras

Andargatchew Messai, diplomat and governor-general of Beghemidir and Simien Province, Ethiopia.[30]

Daughters, Wives, and Titled Societies

In the small-scale societies of precolonial Igboland, eastern Nigeria, leadership and power were not alien to women. Their position was complementary rather than subordinate to that of men. Authority was divided between men and women in a dual-sex political system in which each sex managed and controlled its own affairs. The Igbo had two arms of government, male and female. Female government was further divided into two arms, the *otu umuada* and *otu ndiomu-ala.*

The otu umuada include all married, unmarried, divorced, and widowed daughters of a lineage or community. Meetings are held on a rotating basis between the communities in which the women are married. This resulted in the creation of communication networks of women throughout Igboland. It is these networks that made solidarity between women from vast areas possible during the 1929 Women's War or *Ogu Umunwanyi.*[31]

The otu umuada act as political pressure groups in their natal villages. They create unifying influences between their natal and marital lineages. They settle disputes between women. They also settle intralineage disputes and disputes between their natal villages and the villages in which they are married. In fact, the otu umuada were the supreme court of society. The otu umuada perform rites, rituals, and sacrifices for their community. For instance, they see to the purification rituals of lineage houses and other areas considered polluted so that the gods will not unleash their wrath on people, but will instead provide good health, bounty, and offspring. The otu umuada hear confessions from adulterous wives and perform purification rituals for them and the community.

The otu ndiomu-ala are the wives of the village. Their leader is the most senior wife of the community, the wife who has been married the longest. The otu ndiomu-ala is the medium through which women voice their concerns and protect their interests as wives, mothers, farmers, and traders. Whereas the daughters or otu umuada are the supreme court of society, the otu ndiomu-ala serve as the lower court. They hear and pronounce punishments in cases involving husbands who have mistreated their wives. They make decisions involving the planting and harvesting of crops. They take care of animals that have destroyed women's crops. In addition, the women help lineage wives in times of stress and illness and make sure that the village stream and marketplace are clean. The otu umuada and otu ndiomu-ala form themselves into the Women's Assembly and meet regularly for the good of all women.

Status in Igboland is achieved, not ascribed, and a woman's status is determined by her own achievements, not those of her husband. Women can improve their social standing by taking titles. Igbo women's titles include *ikenga, inachi, inwene, nne mmanwu, otu odu,* and *ikporo.* Titled women are accorded considerable respect and those who show leadership capabilities often hold political office.

In Onitsha, southern Igboland, postmenopausal women can become members of the masquerade society and be addressed by the title "mother of the masquerade" (*nne mmanwu*). Membership in the society accords women prestige and power. They can try cases and enter the house from which the masked spirits emerge. Their presence is required when the *abogo mmuo* (a masked spirit representing young women) appears. Unlike initiation into the masquerade association, a woman can take the *otu odu* (ivory association) title in her natal or affinal village. These women then don heavy ivory bangles and leg jewelry as symbols of their power and clout.

In this chapter, I explore the myriad ways in which African women exhibit political power, authority, and influence within the human political constituency of their various societies. Along the way, I present cases studies from various times and regions of African women's political roles as queens, queen mothers, princesses, and daughters. The underlying theme that connects the histories presented in this chapter is that these women wielded considerable political power and clout in their societies.

In the next chapter, I will consider women of influence and power in the economic realms of their societies, and in particular West Africa's merchant queens.

3

Merchant Queens

African women are known for their economic acumen and often form complex networks of social and commercial relationships with other women and use these networks to empower themselves. They are engaged primarily in local trading, but a few, especially those living in major commercial centers, have established themselves as long-distance traders, or middlepersons.

West African women in particular are noted for their involvement in trade. Virtually all of them are engaged in some type of trade. They trade a variety of items ranging from foodstuffs to ready-made goods. Most monopolize local trade and play a key role in distribution, and some extraordinary women are able to exploit their familial relationships in order to participate in long-distance trade within and outside their communities. This gives the traders, the most successful of whom are merchant queens, greater scope for material accumulation and empowerment than local trade does.

Some West African women are involved in the production of the goods that they sell; others simply sell purchased goods; still others act as middlepersons. Only the extraordinary rise to the status of market or merchant queens. Market activity often brings considerable influence, not only in trade, but in political matters as well, and the female official responsible for the marketplace (e.g., the *omu* among the Igbo, the *iyaloja* among the Yoruba) assumes high political office. In the 1850s and 1860s, Madam Efunroye Tinubu became one of the most important middlepersons operating businesses between Lagos and the Nigerian interior. So did Omu Okwei, the merchant queen of Ossomari, operating around the same time, who was perhaps the most powerful Igbo woman trader of her time. She, like Madam Tinubu, was able to translate her economic clout into political power.

One of the distinguishing features of the economic landscape of precolonial West Africa is that all autonomous precolonial West African societies have their own markets that are linked together by a network of trade routes. These markets are not simply places for buying and selling, but complex, massive networks of contacts and information. There are daily markets and nondaily markets. The nondaily markets are held at four-, five-, or even nine-day intervals, depending on what nation the market is located in. Each West African town, village, or community has at least one daily market. Large towns have several. Markets can also be specialized or nonspecialized; day or night markets. Night markets are not merely places for buying and selling; they are accepted spaces for social life, including celebrations of important occasions, like weddings and funerals, where celebrants can be seen dancing though the marketplace en route to the celebration. Young men and women can also hope to engage in romantic rendezvous at the night market. All West Africa open marketplaces are controlled by women, with women overseeing their running and defining their rules and regulations. In addition, it is women who fix market prices and define market prohibitions.

This chapter explores the power and influence of women commodity traders, association leaders, and leaders of market organizations, courts, and police forces. Case studies of West African merchant queens like the Senegalese *signares* and *métis,* Madam Efunroye Tinubu, Omu Okwei, the market *ahemma* of Asanteland, and nana or mama benzs of Togo and Benin are highlighted.

The *Signares* and *Métis* of Senegal

The title of *signare* (from the Portuguese, *senhora* [madam]), denoting a free woman of property and social consequence, was given to propertied and privileged African or mixed-raced Senegalese women entrepreneurs of the late eighteenth century. These high-class women exercised considerable power, influence, and authority owing to their indigenous-law marriages to European merchants (mainly Portuguese, French, and British), officials, or soldiers who had taken up residence in Senegambian coastal cities during the time of the transatlantic slave trade. Most of these unions were temporary. This was because the European merchants did not as a rule regard the Senegambia region as their permanent homes and would therefore return home to Europe. This notwithstanding, signares were able to leverage their marriages to European men to garner trade goods, gold, landed property, and slaves. They then sold these goods, and from the proceeds were able to sponsor trading expeditions to acquire gold and slaves for themselves. So effective were these signare-controlled entrepreneurial initiatives, that by 1750 the European mercantile companies on the coast started leasing the services of the signares' slaves to provide labor for their projects and lead trade expeditions on their behalf. By so doing, the mercantile companies did not need to acquire their own slaves. Thus, signares played an important role in supporting and reproducing the Senegalese colonial and transnational economy.

Some signares demonstrated their wealth and status by donning gold filigree bracelets, rings, and earrings crafted by Moorish goldsmiths. The wealthiest signares even paid goldsmiths to take up residence with them and craft jewelry exclusively for them. These wealthy signares would also maintain an entourage of slave women as a show of their wealth, propriety, and social standing in society. Some prominent signares included Victoria Albis, Hélène Aussenac, Anne Pépin and her daughter, Anna Colas Pépin, Mary de Saint Jean, Crispina Peres, Cathy Miller, and Bibiana Vuz de França.

Cathy Miller was born of a British father and Senegalese mother and rose to prominence in the town of Saint Louis, Senegal, in the latter part of the eighteenth century. Another signare, Bibiana Vuz de França, was deemed to have become too powerful, that the Portuguese Crown sought ways to wrestle away her power, influence, authority, and wealth. As a result, the Crown falsely accused her of tax evasion and leading a rebellion. She was prosecuted, imprisoned, and then exiled to Cape Verde Islands with her younger brother and another alleged coconspirator.

Yet another signare was so wealthy that she was buying and selling property in Saint-Domingue in the 1770s. Some signares were politically engaged and astute, as was the case of five signares in Gorée, Senegal, who petitioned against a subpar French company that had been granted an exclusive contract on the island.[1]

Whereas signares were African wives or lovers of European men, *métis* were the children of the signares and European merchants or officials who lived in the coastal towns of Saint Louis and Gorée in the eighteenth and early nineteenth centuries. By the 1820s, they had emerged as an absolute oligarchy in Senegal. They were property owners who inherited wealth from their parents and occupied the highest rank in the commercial hierarchy. The métis were able to consolidate their power and wealth because of their connection to the Atlantic commercial system. With the transition from the Atlantic slave trade to legitimate trade in gum, the métis achieved economic success that set them apart from competing Muslim traders. Furthermore, métis middlepersons in the gum-for-guinée trade had more capital than any of their competitors. They owned river-boats. They parlayed their familiarity with the customs of the people of the interior into success in the gum trade. Moreover, their ties with Europeans and prominent Africans improved their influence and credibility, not only with European merchants at the coast, but also with African rulers and traders in the interior.[2]

Nigerian Market or Merchant Queens and Mothers

Among the Yoruba of present-day Nigeria, the *iyaloja,* depending on the context, could be translated into "mother of the market" or "queen." As the "mother of the market," she is the head of the market and of all the women traders. Each Yoruba market, like most West African markets, has a market administration. In the Yoruba market context, under the iyaloja are the market *olosi,* as well as the *aroja* or market keeper, an officer whose duty it is to keep order and manage the market. The aroja actually resides in the marketplace, and the market head, iyaloja, functions not only within the market, but represents the interests of market women in other facets of life.

Efunroye Tinubu

The history of the Yoruba towns of Lagos and Abeo-kuta, Nigeria, is incomplete without Iyaloja Madam

Figure 3.1. Madam Tinubu (ca. 1810–1887), Nigerian business-woman. Photographer unknown, undated.

Efunroye Tinubu. Born in Abeokuta around 1805, she was a prominent trader and a king maker, who would become one of Lagos's most influential women. When she was young, she apprenticed as a trader with her mother and grandmother. She was said to have met an *ifa* (divination) priest, who, because of her kindness, presented Tinubu with an amulet that was believed to have helped position her for large-scale commerce and politics.

Like the signares of the Senegambia region, Madam Tinubu cultivated romantic relationships with politi-cally powerful and astute and influential men, and these relationships, as well as her travel to important cultural and geopolitical frontiers, helped launch her as a politically powerful, savvy, and influential entrepreneur of great status. Tinubu married three men. Her first husband was Prince Adele of Lagos, who died shortly after their wedding. Her second marriage was to King (Oba) Yesufu Bada of Lagos, who was a warrior and Muslim leader. A series of civil conflicts soon displaced Bada, but Tinubu continued to enjoy the prestige and privileges of the royal class. Her third husband, Momoh Bukar, was a noted Arabic scholar.

Efunroye Tinubu played an important role in Lagosian history: she was the wife of a king, the stepmother of another, and the sister-in-law of a third. As Sandra T. Barnes notes, "To each of these rulers she provided political, economic, and military support: protection in exile, backing in succession struggles, and personnel and munitions in military maneuvers. Tinubu did not officially take the queen mother title in Lagos, although she was recognized as the 'power behind the throne'—the only woman in its history for whom a civic monument, Tinubu Square, was named."[3]

In the early 1830s, Tinubu moved to the coastal town of Badagry. When she arrived, there were many wars in the area, which led to an upsurge in the sale of ammunition and arms. With the help of her second husband, Yesufu Bada, she became established in this arms and munitions trade. Tinubu created her own private militia, and because of her prominence as a firearms dealer, she became a powerful player in state affairs. Then she expanded her business to include tobacco, salt, and slaves. She was soon able to assume the lucrative and powerful position as middleperson to the Brazilian slave dealers on the coast. She owned about 360 slaves and oversaw a large household. She established a monopoly in goods brought to Lagos from her hometown, Abeokuta. By the 1850s, she had solidified her position as one of the most prominent and influential members of the commercial elite.[4]

That same decade, Tinubu began trading with Europeans. They trusted her and appreciated her wisdom and influence. As a trusted middleperson who connected the local traders with the Europeans, she was able to build a business monopoly, which in turn boosted her wealth and influence in Lagos so much that the kings and chiefs felt threatened by her. Her estate included great expanses of land and landed properties, as well as kola nut farms.

The kings and chiefs were not the only influential men to be threatened by her. In 1856, Tinubu was driven into exile by the British, who became threatened by her control of the Lagos oba, who had bestowed on her the title of *lyalode*, "mother of the outside." Efunroye Tinubu most certainly benefited from her political networks, but it was her profound business acumen and aggression that made her the wealthiest woman of her time.[5]

In Igboland, Nigeria, the omu and her cabinet of titled women councilors oversee the market and define its rules and regulations. They fix the prices of market goods and define market prohibitions. They also act as a court where those who break market prohibitions and laws are prosecuted and judged. The *awo* (police woman) implements the fixed price regulations. She makes sure that all market taboos are observed; when they are not, she arrests wrongdoers and brings them before the omu court.

Omu Okwei (1872–1943) was a merchant queen from Ossomari, in present-day Nigeria. She was one of the most celebrated, influential, and rich Igbo women of her time. She was born in 1872 to affluent Igbo parents. Her father was Prince Osuna Afubeho, a great warrior and son of King (*Atamanya*) Nzedegwu, who in 1854 negotiated commercial trades with the British. Osuna owned a fleet of war canoes and several hundred slaves. Okwei's mother was a granddaughter of Abo King Obi Ossai, who entered into pacts and treaties with the British as early as the 1830s.

When Okwei was nine years old, her mother sent her to live with her aunt in Igalaland. There, like Efunroye Tinubu before her, she was apprenticed for four years in business, trading in fruits, yams, and poultry. She also learned to speak the Igala language. Her father died when she was fifteen, and she moved back to Atani, a city near the River Niger, to live with her mother.

In 1888, Okwei married the first of two husbands, both of whom her mother strongly disapproved. Joseph Allagoa, from Brass, was one of the most influential traders of his time. She met him at Atani in 1887, while she was trading in palm wine, kola nuts, poultry, and yams. The marriage did not last long. They were divorced a year later, but not before they had a son they named Francis. The young mother sailed the River Niger, and through her first husband's contacts, was able to enter into contracts with European traders and West African agents, whom she supplied with foodstuffs and poultry and in turn bought from them pots, lamps, and clothing.

By 1895, she had remarried. Her second husband was Opene of Abo, whose mother, Okwenu Ezewene (1896–1904), was one of the wealthiest women traders of her day. With Opene, Okwei had a second son they named Peter. Because her husband lived in Onitsha, she transferred her business there and was able to expand her trade in foods to include a retail trade in imported goods like tobacco and cotton merchandise. In 1904, she became an agent for the Niger Delta Company. She shifted her business to palm oil and kernel produce, which she exchanged for imported goods such as gin, matches, pots, and plates. Her dealings with European firms was organized with a credit system of tickets, each of which paid either for 100 measures of oil or for a specific number of trade goods including pans, clothing, tobacco, and enamels. By 1915, she had accumulated large amounts of resources from her retail and produce trade, which she reinvested into her business.

She acquired beautiful girls—children pawned by her debtors—whom she gave out as mistresses or wives to influential non-Igbo businessmen. By so doing, she was able to expand her influence, power, and economic clout to areas as far as Degema, Oguta, Brass, Ndoni, Port Harcourt, and Warri.

Omu Okwei owned landed property and would later work as a money lender. She also worked in the transportation business. Her two sons helped with this. She had given them both the best education available; in 1911, her son Francis Allagoa had become a district interpreter in the Civil Service. By 1917, her second son, Peter Opene, was a storekeeper for the Niger Company at Onitsha.

Despite the fact that she had no formal education, Okwei kept meticulous accounts of her finances. From the 1920s, she started lending money to land litigants. Her rates of interest were exorbitant, ranging from 60 to 90 percent. During the same decade, with the dip in palm oil and kernel prices, Okwei shifted her trade from palm goods to a lucrative trade in gunpowder, ivory, and coral beads. Her influence and power extended far beyond the commercial realm. In 1912, she was made a member of the Native Court and Chief (*eze otu*) of Onitsha Waterside Settlement, a new settlement of about 15,000.

In August 1935, Okwei was given the title of *omu* (queen) of the Ossomari. Her coronation was celebrated with pomp and pageantry, and was attended by representatives of the Hausa, Nupe, Igala, and Abo communities in Onitsha. The omu was coruler with the king; she oversaw women's needs and settled disputes. In addition, she had military, religious, and administrative functions. She was a field marshal whose war canoe led others in all military expeditions.

Omu Okwei also acquired the title of market queen. As market queen, she amassed a fortune, served as chairwoman of the Council of Women, and had a supervisory role over retail trading in the marketplace. She was also responsible for maintaining law and order in the market. Omu Okwei was the last merchant queen to serve in this capacity before the British usurped the authority of the Council of Women in retailing. She died in the town of Onitsha in 1943.[6]

Onokoro Nwa Enyi Nwoti

Trader extraordinaire Onokoro Nwa Enyi Nwoti made a name for herself as a merchant trading in kola nuts, woven textiles, foodstuffs, elephant tusks, horses, and contraband gunpowder. She was born during the first decade of the twentieth century in Aku, Nsukka Division, northern Igboland, Nigeria. She lived with a guardian who raised her and taught her how to trade. By the time she was an adolescent, Onokoro excelled in local trade and was entrusted with finances to start up a long-distance kola nut trade with Igalaland. Onokoro would purchase kola nuts cheaply in her hometown of

Figure 3.2. Madam Onokoro Nwoti. Photograph by Nwando Achebe, Aku, Enugu State, Nigeria, November 8, 1998.

Aku and sneak across the northern border to Igalaland, where she would sell her kola nuts for a huge profit. She bought bags of *okpa* (bambara beans), pepper, *egusi* (Mann's cucumeropsis or white-seed melon), and smoked meat with the proceeds. She kept safe by making her trading journeys with her mentor Ushuabagidi and a band of women traders. They all traveled by lorry. Onokoro Nwoti continued to sell kola nuts long-distance until she married Ezike Anyinwigyi. After her marriage, she channeled the profits of her kola nut business into the palm oil and kernel trade, taking advantage of the British colonial government's promotion of palm produce as the economic core of Igboland's commercial relationship with Europe.

Polygamy allowed wives (especially senior wives) to call upon the support of younger cowives in taking care of their husbands and children. This cooperation and solidarity between cowives allowed senior wives to be away from home for extended periods of time without reneging on family obligations (which would be taken care of by the younger cowife). In return, the senior wife was expected to reciprocate by supplementing her cowife's children's living expenses or providing for their educational needs. Onokoro Nwoti benefited from this institution, marrying wives for her husband (and herself). Moreover, Onokoro Nwoti, who was unable to have biological children of her own, was not burdened with the time-consuming responsibility of taking care of children. This freed her to travel far from home for long periods of time to trade.

Long-distance trade required careful planning, because traders often had to spend several weeks away from their homes. Sometimes the traders traveled to areas outside their cultural and language groups that were potentially dangerous. The traders ensured their safety and security by traveling in groups or bands. Some of these trading bands were made up of as many as thirty women traders. The women traders walked long distances together, stopping from time to time to rest and eat. Onokoro Nwoti took advantage of this female support network, traveling to Igalaland to trade in fish. In addition, Igbo people were governed by a strict code of moral conduct called *omenani*—that which the goddess *ani* decrees to be right or wrong—which controlled the behavior of individuals during these trading expeditions. Being unfaithful to one's spouse was an abomination punishable by insanity and sometimes death; therefore, husbands were assured that their wives would remain faithful to them during long trading trips. Furthermore, itinerant female traders were able to ensure protection from harassment by resting either in their own natal villages, or in the villages of their cowives, if these happened to be on their trade route.

For many years, Onokoro used her trade in kola nuts as a cover to buy and trade contraband gunpowder within and outside Igboland. She traded with Hausa merchants in Onitsha and Europeans in Otumerume. In addition, she was also engaged in trade in woven textiles and snails.

Most long-distance traders in Nsukka Division traveled to their destinations by land. However, on occasion Onokoro Nwoti and her band of female trader friends made their trading journeys by canoe across the River Niger. She often carried foodstuffs, seasoning, and woven cloth. By the mid-1950s, Onokoro Nwoti had distinguished herself as a food and cloth trader. She then was eager to explore new trading ventures.

The next direction that Onokoro Nwoti took her trading was to tap into the important, costly, and male-dominated trade in horses and elephant tusks. Onokoro Nwoti's entry into this male trading enterprise solidified her position as the female trader extraordinaire of Aku, Nsukka Division. She bought horses at the famed horse market in Ibagwa and elephant tusks from itinerant Agu Ukwu traders. In fact, by the mid- to late 1950s, Onokoro Nwoti had accumulated so much money that she was able to treat her husband and herself to a luxurious Mercedes-Benz automobile. Onokoro Nwoti used the rewards of her trading to splurge on her loved ones and herself. She not only took titles for herself, but also inducted her "wives" and male friends into Aku's elite title societies.

Between 1951 and 1960, three parties—the Action Group (AG), the Northern Peoples' Congress (NPC), and the National Council of Nigeria and the Cameroons (NCNC)—dominated the political life of Nigeria. The Action Group was controlled almost entirely by the Yoruba south, the Northern Peoples' Congress by the Hausa north, and the National Council of Nigeria and the Cameroons by the Igbo east. A staunch member of the NCNC, as well as its women's leader in Aku, Onokoro Nwoti was able to promote the nationalist agenda of her party at the grassroots level. She channeled much of her economic and political clout into gathering Aku women's support for the NCNC party and its leader Nnamdi Azikiwe, for whom she campaigned tirelessly. Although she was in her midnineties in 1998 and had drastically reduced her long-distance travels, Onokoro Nwoti remained active in buying and selling kola nuts in nearby marketplaces, living out her days as a merchant queen of substance.

Ghanaian Market Queens:
The Ahemmas of Asanteland

In Kumasi Central Market, in present-day Ghana, the market queen of the traders' association goes by the title *ohemaa*. There are several *ahemaa* (plural) operating in Kumasi Central Market, and each leads a group of commodity traders. Thus, there is an ohemaa for foodstuff traders and an ohemaa for nonperishable goods traders. There are even ahemaa for specific commodities: for instance, an ohemaa for plantains and an ohemaa for tomatoes. Each ohemaa has total authority over her own commodity group. She does not consult the other ahemaa about issues related to her own commodity group and rejects any interference from them. The market ohemaa is a manager whose duties include maintaining harmony within the traders' association, partnering with other market queens to manage the entire market, and negotiating favorable terms with stakeholders.

In the Kumasi Central Market, the head of the yam traders, the *bayerehemaa,* has seniority over all the other ahemaa, and she takes the lead in joint actions among ahemaa. In the coastal markets in Accra, the leader of the collective ahemaa is the ohemaa of the cloth traders. On ceremonial occasions, or when in negotiation with officials, the Kumasi Central Market bayerehemaa leads the delegation of ahemaa and speaks for them. The ahemaa of yams, cassavas, tomatoes, *kontonmere* (taro leaves), cocoyams, oranges, and snail produce constitute a sect of senior ahemaa called *ahemaafo,* who consult with one another about market affairs. For example, bayerehemaa cannot make a major decision without consulting the senior ahemaa. Following Asante decision-making norms, the bayerehemaa listens to each speak, and considers their contributions in her decision-making. The ahemaafo represents Kumasi Central Market traders as a whole in negotiations with the market manager and nontraders during periods of crisis—such as the price control enforcements of 1979—and peace.[7]

In large market centers, such as the Kumasi Central Market and the Navrongo Market, ahemaa tap into complex familial and clientele networks for their success, authority, and influence. These networks are inseparable and feed off each other. For instance, Auntie Afriyie's rise to the queen of palm nuts was as a result of her hard work and shrewdness. She shadowed incumbent palm nut queens, often volunteering to perform many of their duties. When the incumbent queen died, she became the most suitable candidate for the position.[8]

Madam Okesie

Okesie, whose name literally translates into "the big one" in Twi, is a forty-nine-year-old plantain market queen. Okesie lives up to her name with regard to her size as well as the power and influence she has within the marketplace. She is one of the founders of a market on the outskirts of Accra. Though small, the market offers a good mix of commodities for the discerning shopper. Okesie's primary concern as a plantain market queen and wholesaler is that her fellow plantain sellers are able to secure enough plantains, at good prices, to sell to their customers throughout the year, especially because the small market is often in competition with the larger Tema and Agbogbloshie markets, which have the most plantains in the area.

She is able to secure the plantains she needs by maintaining lines of communication with her suppliers. She checks on them regularly, inquiring about their health, families, and welfare. Having developed these relationships with her suppliers, she can rely on them to bring in plantains when plantains are plentiful—and even when they are scarce: "[I] find out how they are faring . . . [so that] if [plantains] abound, [the supplier] brings it to [me], and when it is scarce too, he brings it."[9]

Okesie uses her mobile phone to maintain direct contact with plantain farmers, whose farms tend to be far from the market in remote villages. She lays out the welcome mat when these farmer-suppliers travel from their farming villages to the city to sell their produce to the market women. She maintains the loyalty of her suppliers by routinely throwing in additional services and assistance, free of charge, when they arrive with their goods. For instance, she makes sure that the farmers are fed and provides whatever help they need in securing commodities they would like to take back to their village homes. In short, Market Queen Okesie must distinguish herself and her market, not only by the price that she is willing to offer farmer-suppliers, but also in the kind of hospitality service that she provides. Okesie explains: "I have to settle [meaning make happy] her [the farmer] very fine. And when she is leaving, [I] have to give her something . . . [I] will buy soap. [I] have to treat the person nicely, if [I] don't, she will not bring the goods because there are so many markets where they will treat her nicely if she takes it there."

In the plantain trade, the price of plantains is low during the plantain season in August, and high when plantains are not in season. As an influential and authoritative plantain market mother, Okesie's main concern is ensuring that a steady supply of plantains, at reasonable prices, reaches her market all year long. Without plantains to sell, the plantain market women are unable to make any money.[10]

Madam Abena

In the major shopping district of central Accra is the Makola market, where Abena, a middle-aged wife and mother of three, sells cloth from inside her shop—a concrete building situated in the prime spot in the market. The ten-year lease on the shop cost her 30,000 Ghanaian cedis (approximately $15,300).

Market Queen Abena was born into privilege. Her father was a wholesaler of Dutch-made Vlisco cloth, called Hollandis or Hollandais (see the section, below, on *mama* or *nana benzs* for a discussion of Vlisco cloth), and made a fortune doing so. He was a polygamist, who married nine wives and had seventeen children. And because he was so rich, his daughter Abena benefited from being able to complete postsecondary education in a vocational training institute. She then worked as a bank teller for Barclays Bank. Her days at Barclays were, however, short lived. She soon decided to try her hand at the family cloth business, and started to export Ghanaian food to London, which she exchanged for the highest-quality imported cloth from Holland, as well as cheaper cloth from China.

Having made a fortune herself, Market Queen Abena was able to send all three of her children to one of the most elite and expensive private universities in Ghana, Ashesi University. A smart businesswoman, Abena is Internet savvy and incorporates mobile technologies—including mobile banking and money transfers—into her business to efficiently and effectively manage her inventory, sales, and ledgers.[11]

Mama or Nana Benzs of Lomé, Togo

As previously discussed, West African markets are dominated by powerful and influential women who control prices and determine who can buy their goods. Throughout West Africa, from Senegal to Côte d'Ivoire, to Togo to

Cameroon, the most influential, powerful, and wealthy of these women entrepreneurs are affectionately referred to as *mama benz* or *nana benz,* a title bestowed on them because each has several chauffeur-driven Mercedes-Benzs. In particular, mama benz is a name given to an exclusive club of women who control the sale of printed African textiles and have made a fortune selling Dutch-made Vlisco, also known as Hollandis (also spelled Hollandais) or the "Real Dutch Wax." These textiles are marketed under local names such as "Capable Woman," "Eye of My Rival," "If My Husband Goes Out, I Go Out, Too," "Dallas," "Endless Love," and "Honey, Don't Turn Your Back." These enterprising and flamboyant market queens of Vlisco cloth are rich and successful—many have become millionaires several times over, buying palatial mansions and other real estate in Africa, Europe, and America; owning fleets of expensive luxury cars and taxis; owning empires of high-class restaurants and bakeries; sending their children to expensive private finishing schools in Europe and America; and vacationing in the world's most expensive and exclusive spots.

Vlisco, which was founded in 1846, is a Dutch company that produces expensive colorful printed textiles that are popular in West Africa, especially among the upper and middle classes. Manufactured in the Netherlands, Vlisco fabrics have been transported to West Africa for more than 160 years. By the 1960s, Vlisco had become the exclusive supplier of textiles for the West

African market. And, in keeping with the traditional role of West African women as traders, the Vlisco company contracted local women to sell their textiles. This was, however, not always the case: earlier in their history of distribution in West Africa, Vlisco had contracted Dutch men, otherwise known as "Vlisco Men," some of whom would, like the European partners of the Senegambia signares before them, visit West Africa for given periods of time and cultivate temporary relationships with local West African women. These "Vlisco Men" did not last the test of time, and West African female entrepreneurs were able to solidify their control of this Vlisco luxury brand as market leaders with greatest prestige.

Vlisco women successfully parlayed their extensive wealth into political, social, and cultural power, authority, and influence. In Togo, they became a major contributor to the country's only legal political party, and subsequently objected to a proposal by the government to raise textile import tariffs. Their power and clout were evidenced when as a result of these objections, President Gnassingbe Eyadema (1967–2005) kept these tariffs low. When Togolese economists suggested that the government institute price controls, Mr. Eyadema indignantly responded, "The Nana Benz are the seat on which the Government stands. We must not disturb them."[12] In return, when President Eyadema was short a few limousines for visiting heads of state, the nana benzs came to the rescue. In fact, some mama benzs were said to have loaned thirty Mercedes-Benzs to chauffeur important state visitors. So prestigious and influential was the title of "mama benz" that an important fashion magazine in Toronto, Canada, bears its name.[13]

Maggy Lawson

Mama Benz Maggy Lawson of Lomé, Togo, grew rich by trading in brightly printed cotton cloth known as *pagnes* from which West African men, women, and children have garments made. In fact, Maggy Lawson descends from a line of market queens. Her mother, Madam Lawson, Sr., was said to have coined the term "mama benz," which was attributed to the fact that she was the first wholesaler in Lomé to buy the German luxury car. The senior Madam Lawson could neither read nor write but worked her way up to become a multimillionaire.

She grew up in rural Togo, in modest circumstances, and was one of many siblings. When she was young, she moved to Lomé, the capital city, and sold textiles there. She taught herself to speak French and English, and as a trader, was able to commit hundreds of fabric designs and their cost to memory. The senior Lawson then parlayed her hard work into becoming one of the most privileged wholesalers of Vlisco ever known in Lomé. She was even able to secure the exclusive right to sell certain Vlisco patterns. Until her death in 2004, Madam Lawson, Sr., woke up every morning at 4 A.M.

Maggy Lawson carries on her mother's legacy. She is one of fifteen formidable, powerful, influential, and savvy women who control Togo's cloth trade. She also drives a Mercedes-Benz and orders fabric from Vlisco. Mama Benz Maggy Lawson exemplifies opulence. She wears 14-carat gold-framed glasses and carries Chanel handbags. Maggy Lawson owns homes in the United States (Dallas and Washington, DC), Paris, the Côte d'Azur, and Monaco. She also owns a villa on the out-skirts of Lomé finished with marble and teak paneling. She is wealthy, influential, and politically powerful, rep-resenting the coastal regions in the Togolese Parliament and advising the minister of labor on important eco-nomic questions.

Maggy Lawson is also an international textile trader who owns several warehouses and employs numerous workers. She sells her textiles to foreign dealers from Benin, Burkina Faso, and Nigeria, who in turn pay de-posits to her in advance of the materials arriving. Lomé market women mostly operate on credit and pay Maggy Lawson interest. Maggy Lawson's business is based on trust, longstanding relationships, and a network that spans all of West and Central Africa.

In the 1980s, Togo was a stable and flourishing country. In the early 1990s, political unrest led to major inflation. Within a short time, the cost of goods dou-bled, and people could no longer afford Vlisco. Because of deteriorating market conditions, and to escape her dependence on the Dutch company, Maggy Lawson was forced to adjust her sales strategy. She still brought in the imported Vlisco products but sold them only to the

Figure 3.3. A textile merchant presents her colorful fabrics in Togo. Photograph by Alexander Sarlay, August 16, 2016.

elite. She then started to produce fabrics for the everyday people. Mama Benz Maggy Lawson's collection is called Manatex. A quarter the cost of Vlisco, the collection mimics the designs of the more expensive Vlisco and is made in China. The fabric is thinner and slightly paler than its more expensive counterpart. Moreover, it does not hold up as well to laundering. Nonetheless, one of her more famous and lucrative Manatex designs—a design for which she earned several hundred thousand Swiss francs—feature the portraits of all the former presidents of Togo. By producing her own Manatex line, Mama Benz is not only emancipating herself from Vlisco, she has effectively established herself as a powerful and influential textile designer and manufacturer who is able to shape the tastes of her consumers and control the market.[14]

In neighboring Cotonou, Benin Republic, a new group of Beninese women wholesalers has emerged. They are young, some are educated, and IT-savvy. Unlike the vast majority of the Togolese Mama Benzs before them, these new Beninese market queens have concerned themselves not with selling expensive Vlisco Dutch waxes but with targeting the needs of a broad segment of the Beninese population—the everyday people—who can only afford low-price wax fabrics. Like Mama Benz Lawson, these Mama Benzs have ingeniously worked to dominate the import market for low-priced Chinese waxes; but they also control the Indian and other Asian-made waxes, which began entering the African textile market in the mid-1990s. As discussed above, these cheaper brands were often copies of the more expensive Vlisco cloth. At the famous Dantokpa market, the textile shops located in Missébo neighborhood, and the Hagi Ali Shopping Centre, are filled with Asian copies of the wax fabrics that now dominate the trade, overshadowing the over-priced textiles of the wealthy, Vlisco Dutch Wax, which is fast losing its market share.

Today these cheaply produced fabrics from Asia dominate the wholesale market in most West African market towns, from Lomé, to Cotonou, to Abidjan, to Dakar, and Accra. Thus, these Beninese mama benzs have leveraged their success in the import trade in cheap textiles to establish personal local and global networks that incorporate small retailers, street vendors, and more established middlepersons.

Justine Chodaton

The predecessors of these new age Beninese mama benzs, an older generation of mama benzs, had organized themselves into a market women's group known as the Union Nationale des Commerçantes du Bénin (UNACOBE). The most powerful of UNACOBE's leaders were mama benzs Augustine Codjia, Grace Lawani, and Justine Chodaton. These mama benzs also distinguished themselves by having been elected to the Cotonou Chamber of Commerce. They were powerful and influential, and they represented competing political and business networks. Mama Benz Justine Chodaton, for instance, was able to organize groups of market women into her personal trade network. She did this by first creating two groups, the Groupement Professionnel des Vendeuses des Marchés du Bénin (GPVMB) and in 1992 the Syndicat National des Vendeuses et des Vendeurs et Assimilés des Marchés du Bénin (SYNAVAMAB). Mama Benz Chodaton is therefore an example of a market queen who successfully developed economic, social, and political clout and built an impressive arsenal of economic resources that she was able to convert into social and political capital. A renaissance woman among Benin tradeswomen and an activist for several years, the Honorable Justine Chodaton would become an elected member of the second, third, fourth, and fifth Beninese legislatures.

Justine Chodaton was born in 1935 in Adja Tado, a western Benin town bordering Togo, into a prominent merchant family in Whydah, Benin. She moved to the Benin capital city of Abomey when she was twelve years old. Her grandmother and mother were traders, and it was they who taught her how to trade. In 1956, Chodaton married and started selling African textiles in Cotonou, Benin's largest city and economic capital. At that time, her net worth was 15,000 francs, and with that money she became an international trader. She bought textiles from Lomé, Togo, and Accra, Ghana, and then sold them for a profit in Benin. Her international textile business was so successful that after three years she was able to purchase two parcels of land and a Mercedes-Benz. She also bought a luxury home. When the local agent of Vlisco set up in Cotonou, Chodaton began buying Dutch wax textiles directly from the Vlisco agent and stopped traveling to Lomé and Accra.

In the 1960s, Chodaton set up networks in trade and politics. She set up a trade network of retailers to defend the business interests of Beninese market women and offer mutual assistance during times of difficulty. Her network was influential and powerful and controlled the trade in Dutch wax textiles at Dantokpa market, setting the rules for trade and creating a monopoly that lasted several years. A tested trade leader, Chodaton was often asked to help reorganize market associations in Benin and elsewhere. She thus acquired skills in conflict mediation and resolution, like the Igbo omus and the Yoruba iyalojas discussed earlier.

Chodaton also set up a credit system for Beninese women traders. Harnessing her influence with the director of the Beninese national textile company, Société Beninoise de Textiles SA (SOBETEX), and the representative of Vlisco in Cotonou, Chodaton extended credit to local vendors, who were expected to pay her back (with substantial interest) after they had sold their textiles. During this time, Chodaton was not only a mama benz but also the leader of all the Dutch wax textile wholesalers, who could not make any decisions without her consent.

Chodaton was able to parlay her credit-giving enterprise into political clout and strongly encouraged her clients to support her political goals. Moreover, either the credit that Chodaton distributed to male and female traders had to be paid back with interest or new credit had to be taken from her in the form of commodities. This system ensured that traders who came to her for credit became dependent on her.

Although illiterate, Chodaton was a skilled organizer and leader. She transformed her social network into GPVMB, a formal professional marketing association whose aim it was to reach market women throughout Benin. In 1960, through this organization, Chodaton was able to organize a resistance against President Hubert Maga, who had jailed some of the women traders. And as the president of the retailers' groups UNACOBE and later, SYNAVAMAB, she was able to parlay her clout and influence into being elected three times to national parliament.[15]

In this chapter, I have documented the lives and worlds of the West African merchant queens known as market queens and mama or nana benzs. Each woman was and is exceptional in that she reached the pinnacle of her chosen profession, whether it be as a kola nut, plantain, gunpowder, or textile trader.

In chapter 4, I chronicle the lives of seven women leaders who ruled as headmen, kings, and paramount chiefs. Their stories highlight the flexibility and fluidity of the African gender system, which allows women to assume the gendered role of men and rule as men.

4

Female Headmen, Kings, and Paramount Chiefs

In Africa, sex and gender do not coincide; instead, gender is flexible and fluid, allowing women to become men, and men, women, thus creating unique African categories such as *female* husband, *female* son, and *male* priestess. The flexibility and fluidity of gender roles translate into leadership. Some exceptional African women have been able to transform themselves into gendered men in order to rule their societies, not as princesses or queens, but as headmen, paramount chiefs, and kings. In this chapter I present case studies of exceptional women who ruled as men and explore the conditions that supported, reinforced, and/or extended the contours of such gender transformation leadership. The rulers profiled include Hatshepsut, who dressed and ruled as pharaoh; Ebulejonu, the first *attah* or *female* king of the Igala monarchy; King Nzingha of Ndongo, who also dressed as a man and forbade her subjects to call her queen; King Naa Dode Akabi of the Galand, Ghana; Headman Wangu wa Makeri of Gĩkũyũland, colonial Kenya; Ahebi Ugbabe, the *female* king of colonial Nigeria; and Paramount Chief Mosadi Seboko of the Balete people of Botswana.

Pharaoh Hatshepsut

Although her historical existence is questionable, the *female* pharaoh Nitocris, purportedly the sister of Merenre Nemtyemsaf II and the daughter of Pepi II and Queen Neith, may have been the last pharaoh to rule Egypt in the Sixth Dynasty (ca. 2345–2181 BCE), Old Kingdom.[1] However, as many as five other women are believed to have ruled in the Early Dynastic Period, as early as the First Dynasty. More is known about Sobekneferu, "the beauty of Sobek" (the crocodile god), who was the first *female* pharoah for whose reign physical evidence survives. She ruled in the late nineteenth century BCE as the last pharaoh in the Twelfth Dynasty, after the death of Amenemhat IV. Sobekneferu most frequently used feminine titles, but she combined both male and female elements in her dress and regalia.[2] Hatshepsut, who reigned between ca. 1478 and 1458 BCE, the "foremost of noble ladies," is widely regarded as one of Egypt's most successful *female* pharaohs. She dressed as a man, had herself portrayed as male, and ordered her subjects to refer to her as king.[3]

As the fifth pharaoh of the Eighteenth Dynasty, Hatshepsut was crowned pharaoh around 1478 BCE. Referred to as "the first great woman in history of whom we are informed,"[4] Hatshepsut was the only child of King Thutmose I and his wife, Queen Ahmose.

Hatshepsut was twelve when her father died. Shortly after her father's death, she married her half-brother Thutmose II, the son of Mutnofret, and became queen. Thutmose and Hatshepsut had a daughter, Neferure, and Thutmose also had a son by his concubine, Isis. Thutmose II died fifteen years after he and Hatshepsut were married, and his infant son by Isis, Thutmose III, became heir apparent. As Thutmose III was too young to assume the throne, Hatshepsut stepped in as regent, an office that she occupied during the first six years of the stepmother/stepson rule. By the end of their seventh year of joint rule, however, Hatshepsut was crowned pharaoh. The full titles of pharaoh were bestowed on her, and Hatshepsut adopted the dress of male rulers, including a *shendyt* kilt, *nemes* headdress with its *uraeus* and *khat* head cloth, and a false beard. Because it was unusal for the Egyptians to have a female pharaoh, Hatshepsut had her likeness depicted as male, and this directive helped uphold her authority and place as pharaoh.

Hatshepsut was a charismatic ruler and a masterful politician and stateswoman. She surrounded herself with a group of loyal officials, including Senenmut, who helped her successfully run the kingdom. Senenmut was in charge of all royal works. He also served as a tutor to Hatshepsut's daughter, Neferure. Hatshepsut's reign ushered in a peaceful time in Egypt's history, and as a result, Egypt prospered. During her rule, Hatshepsut sent several trade expeditions abroad, including one to Punt in present-day Somalia that returned with gold, ebony, ivory, spices, animal skins, baboons, and processed and living myrrh trees.

Hatshepsut also launched an extensive building and restoration program in Egypt, constructing several temples, including one to honor the national god *amon-re* in Thebes and a rock temple in Middle Egypt, known to the Greeks as Speos Artemidos. Hatshepsut also had the Al-Karnak temple remodeled, adding pillars to it, in addition to the Red Chapel.

Her greatest architectural accomplishment, however, was the construction of the Dayr al-Baḥrī temple, which was also named for amon-re. This magnificent temple included chapels dedicated to the royal ancestors and a number of significant Egyptian deities. When

Figure 4.1. The Temple of Hatshepsut in Luxor. Photograph by Andrea Piroddi, undated.

Hatshepsut died in 1458 BCE, she was interred in the Valley of the Kings next to her father.[5]

Attah-Ebulejonu

In Igalaland, in present-day southeastern Nigeria, one of the earliest *attah*-Igalas (kings of the Igala) was a woman, Ebulejonu ("woman who became chief or king"). Known as Ebule, and reigning in the sixteenth century, she was Igalaland's first and last female king. The Igala monarchy, among the oldest and most powerful kingdoms in central Nigeria, centers around the office of the attah-Igala, who was regarded as the "father" of all Igala people.

According to the Wukari tradition of Igala kingship origin, Attah-Ebulejonu's father, Attah-Abutu Eje, was half-human and half-leopard. The king of Wukari, so tradition holds, had a daughter who collected firewood from the forest every day. One day, the king's daughter was confronted by a leopard. Terrified, the king's daughter was transfixed to the spot, where before her eyes the leopard metamorphosed into a handsome young man. The princess was instantaneously enamored and captivated by this young man's magnetism, and as a result, she trekked to the same spot daily to see him. Soon, according to the tradition, the two lovebirds decided to get married. Once the princess informed her parents about her love interest, the king and queen wanted to meet him. Thus, a few days later, the princess took them into the forest. Her handsome suitor once again appeared as a leopard, causing the king and queen to take flight.

However, the love-struck princess remained undeterred. She continued to visit her "prince," and in time their love was consummated and the princess gave birth to a baby boy they named Abutu Eje ("Leopard" in Igala).

Abutu Eje grew up in Wukari to become a man of great courage and charm. His insecure father-in-law king, however, drove him away because he feared that Abutu Eje might usurp his throne. In consequence, Abutu Eje wandered away to Idah, where he established a royal throne. And because he was so powerful, Abutu Eje was able to sufficiently impress the Igala people, so that they addressed him as *attah* (father). Another version of this tradition states that Abutu Eje did not make it to Igalaland, but died en route to Igalaland, thus paving the way for his only child, Ebule, to rule as *female* king.

Leopard symbolism, in the form of a leopard emblem, has survived to the present day in Igala political life and represents the oldest demonstration of power and authority in the Igala kingdom. It also features prominently during the burial ceremonies of the attah, in addition to individuals related to the king.

The attah-Igala had as a counterpart the *achadu,* who functioned as a sort of prime minister. The achadu was the leader of the *Igala mela* or the nine traditional groups that had first settled in Idah. According to tradition, Attah-Ebulejonu's achadu was an outsider, an Igbo hunter of "slave" origin called Acho Omeppa who was captured and brought before the *female* king Ebulejonu.

King Ebule, captivated by Acho, decided to spare his life. Then, to the dismay of her subjects, she befriended this man of lowly status. Her horrified subjects branded this man with the name "achadu," meaning "Acho the slave." Nonetheless, King Ebulejonu remained steadfast in her love for the Igbo "slave," Acho Omeppa, and she later married him. However, because Omeppa was a keen hunter, he would not live with Ebulejonu. He instead built a compound for her close to him, so that he could resume his hunting activities in surrounding locales.

After Attah-Ebulejonu died, her brother, Agenapoje, asked her husband, Achadu Omeppa, to transfer Ebule's title to him because she had not given birth to any children of her own. Omeppa agreed, but only if Agenapoje perforated his ears like Ebule, the *female* king. The act of perforating one's ears could be read as a gendered modification—from overt masculine king to a tempered king with female traits. The soon-to-be male king would be expected to adopt the quintessence of Omeppa's *female* king wife, Ebulejonu, to embody the true essence of the *female* king. This tradition of ear perforation remains in practice today. The office of attah is validated by the performance of this ancient ritual.

It is a paradox that Attah-Ebulejonu, like Hatshepsut of Egypt before her, ruled as a king, not a queen, and is remembered that way today. This perhaps helped set the precedent for the coronation of another Nigerian woman, Ahebi Ugbabe, who ruled as king about four centuries later.[6]

King Naa Dode Akabi

Among the Ga of present-day central Ghana lived a young and beautiful girl. Her name was Akabi and she adorned herself in beautiful clothing and ornaments. And wherever she went, she was accompanied by two maidens as beautiful as she. Akabi also possessed masculine attributes. She was physically strong, taller than the average man, and competitive with boys in hunting and wrestling. She also competed with boys in holding hot roasted yams, jumping over fire, and catching live animals.

Ga oral sources describe Naa Dode Akabi as masculine, a "he-woman" (a man in a female body). She made her entry into the Ga historical records during the reign of Mantse Mampong Okai (ca. 1600–1642), the great-grandson of Ayi Kushi and Naa Dode's spouse. They had a son named Okaikoi (d. 1677); and Mantse Mampong Okai, Naa Dode, and their son, Mantse Okaikoi, reigned consecutively in the Ga capital of Ayawaso between ca. 1600 and 1680.

Records indicate that Naa Dode's marriage to the much older Mantse Mampong Okai was a marriage of convenience. After his death, Naa Dode strove to gain leadership of the Gamei or Ga peoples to safeguard her young son's rights to the throne in the face of the competing interests of his three half-brothers. Thus, Naa Dode's ascent to the throne was driven by motherhood and maternal instinct. She was an intelligent woman who took possession of her late husband's property and usurped his government so that after her death her young son, Prince Okaikoi, could ascend to the throne.

Naa Dode's rise to power was contested by the Ga male gerontocracy, who had previously settled on a different male regent for the kingdom after Mantse Mampong Okai's death. But Naa Dode Akabi, through guile and wisdom, succeeded in convincing them that she was a more suitable candidate to rule the kingdom. Naa Dode secured her power, ruling both the Obutu and the Ga peoples of central Ghana.

Naa Dode Akabi is remembered in oral tradition as a cruel and tyrannical regent who ruled over the Gamei with a fierce hand. So cruel was she said to have been, that when she ordered her subjugated subjects to dig a deep well, her subjects lured Naa Dode Akabi into the incomplete shaft and buried her alive. The manner in which the subjugated Ga people killed their tyrannical leader, Naa Dode, has survived today in the mode of the ritual burial of animals or powerful medicines to ward off impending epidemics, war, death, or any other misfortune.[7]

King Nzingha

In 1623, at the age of forty-one, Nzingha became the ruler of Ndongo, in present-day Angola. Like Hatshepsut, she forbade her Mbundu subjects from calling her queen; she insisted on being called king and went into battle dressed like a man. Nzingha was born in the late 1580s, one of five children of the *ngola* (king) Kiluanji.

When the princess came of age, she married and had a son. Her father was a tyrannical leader, who as a consequence was deposed and killed. His oldest illegitimate son, Mbanda, then installed himself as ngola. Mbanda subsequently rid the kingdom of all opposition (real and imagined), killing his nephew, Nzingha's only child, in the process. Spurred on by paranoia, he even killed many chiefs who had supported his ascension to the throne. As a result, Nzingha fled Mbandi, the Ndongo capital, with her husband and sisters, and settled in neighboring Matamba.

It was against this backdrop that the Portuguese appeared, advancing into the kingdom while searching for silver mines. Unable to withstand the Portuguese advance, Nzingha's brother, Mbanda, fled, surrendering the heartland to the foreign invaders. He would retreat to an island on the Cuanza River. Once there he asked Nzingha to help him negotiate a peace treaty with the Portuguese. Because the hostility between sister and brother was real, Nzingha only consented to do so for love of nation. Even though Mbanda had surrendered everything to the Portuguese, the natural diplomat Nzingha was not deterred. She made her way to the governor's residence, surrounded by musicians heralding her approach, and flanked by her serving women. Upon her arrival, she discovered that there was only one seat in the receiving room, meant for Portuguese governor João Correa da Souza. This meant that Nzingha would have to sit on the floor like a commoner. Nzingha,

Figure 4.2. King Nzingha, 1657. Photographer unknown, undated.

intercepting this would-be insult, instructed one of her serving women to kneel on all fours, thus creating a human seat for the princess to sit on. She then ensconced herself with much regality and authority, heralding an atmosphere of equality that would foreshadow the negotiations to come. When Correa da Souza asked for the return of all Portuguese prisoners taken by the Mbundu, Nzingha cunningly agreed, but with the caveat that all the Mbundu prisoners sold and sent away to Brazil and other regions be returned to them in exchange, thus creating an impasse. In the end, the Portuguese were forced to sign a treaty recognizing Ngola Mbandi as ruler of the independent Ndongo kingdom and promised to withdraw their army. The Ndongo, on their part, promised to return all Portuguese prisoners, aid the Portuguese in acquiring slaves for the Atlantic trade, and help them in resisting their common enemy, the Jaga.

It might have been Correa da Souza's intent to hold up his own end of the bargain, but pressure from Lisbon and Brazil to increase the enslavement of human beings demanded that the peoples of Ndongo be fair game. When the governor, in an ill-advised move, sent an African convert to Ndongo instead of honoring his promise to supply the Portuguese priest that the people had requested, the Ndongo saw this move as an indication that the Portuguese were going to renege on their promise to return their people to them. Nzingha pleaded with her brother to fight for the return of their kingdom, but he was not interested in fighting the Portuguese. Nzingha, now convinced that she must not only fight the Portuguese to recover their lands but also dethrone her treacherous and weak brother, formed an alliance with the much-feared Jaga. Together they built an army of guerrilla fighters that included many murderers. They captured Mbanda's son and poisoned him. This was the beginning of a series of wars that Nzingha waged to rid her kingdom of the slave-raiding Portuguese and return Ndongo to its rightful owners.

The struggle was extremely costly for Nzingha, who fought the Portuguese all her life, suffering severe setbacks: one sister was strangled by the Portuguese, another imprisoned. Nzingha died on December 17, 1663, at the age of about eighty-two; the nation that she had fought so hard to defend survived her. Although Nzingha failed in her mission to expel the Portuguese, her historic importance transcends this failure; she awakened and encouraged the first known stirring of nationalism in West Central Africa.[8]

Headman Wangu wa Makeri

Wangu wa Makeri (ca. 1850–1936) was born to Gĩkũyũ parents, Gatuika Macharia and Wakeru, around 1850, in the village of Gitie in the present-day Central Province of Kenya. She had no formal education but worked on her parent's farm when she was young. It was during this time that she met her future husband, Makeri wa Mbogo. They soon married and had six children.

In 1902, Wangu wa Makeri was appointed to the office of headman of Weithaga in Kangema Division, by a British proxy, Kanuri wa Gakure, chief of Fort Hall, now Murang'a. She was the only woman in Kenya to have be so appointed, partly as payback for an affair she was having with wa Gakure.

That notwithstanding, Wangu wa Makeri's service record was impressive. As a headman, she acted as an intermediary between her people and the British colonial masters, especially during the period of taxation. However, in spite of her solid leadership record, wa Makeri was forced to resign in June 1909. She was forced out of office because she and Karuri wa Gakure, with whom she had continued to enjoy an adulterous relationship, had committed the gaffe of dancing the *kibata*—an exclusive dance for male warriors—while naked.

Wangu wa Makeri had also been accused of behaving like a man. She had been instrumental in arranging for her husband, Makeri, to marry seven other wives, in order to free herself from her marital obligations. She was also a *female* husband, who married two women for herself as a show of machismo and clout.[9]

King Ahebi Ugbabe

Ahebi Ugbabe was born during the latter part of the nineteenth century in Enugu-Ezike, northern Igboland, Nigeria. When she was young, she lived with her mother's relatives in a town called Unadu. She later returned to her father's village and within the space of a few years escaped to Igalaland. Here is what happened: When Ahebi Ugbabe was young, her family started experiencing misfortune. Ahebi's father, in an attempt to trace the origins of these ill fortunes, sought out the expertise of a diviner. The seer soon revealed the mysteries of his divination: in order for things to get better, Ahebi would have to be offered as a living sacrifice to appease the great goddess, *ohe*. Ahebi refused to be dedicated. Her actions pitted her against society, and as a result she was forced to flee Enugu-Ezike.

She was driven into exile to Igalaland, where she was thrown into a vicious and harsh reality. She became a sex worker. Ahebi Ugbabe used this form of work to her advantage. She traveled widely and learned to speak many languages, including Igala, Nupe, and Pidgin English. Her profession put her in touch with a number of prominent citizens, including some British colonialists and the *attah* or king of Igalaland, whose power extended into northern Igboland.

By the mid-1910s, Ahebi Ugbabe decided to accompany the British invaders back to her natal town. Immediately following her return to Enugu-Ezike, Ahebi allied herself with the political elite. Her linguistic skills gave her access to British colonial officers. Ever ambitious, and talented, Ahebi recognized in the British new opportunities for political power and clout that had not existed in the same way in the precolonial order. The office of warrant chief became a promise of individualized political might that remained unavailable to women elsewhere in British colonial Africa. In October 1918, the British made Ahebi warrant chief (and like wa Makeri before her, she had previously been named headman).

Once appointed, a divide developed between Ahebi and the recognized leadership of male elders. The male ruling elite wanted no part in Ahebi's political ascent but found that they did not have a choice in the matter because the British stood firmly behind Ahebi. This European support was, however, not enough to satisfy Ahebi. She mounted a vigorous campaign to become *eze* (king) in order to further cement her position in government and society.

As king and warrant chief, Ahebi turned her palace into a court, where she settled cases between individuals and obtained money for the services. Ahebi's palace was also a sanctuary for runaway women. Ahebi married some of women who decided to stay, consequently becoming their *female* husband.

Figure 4.3. King Ahebi Ugbabe's insignia of office. Photograph by Nwando Achebe, Umuida, Enugu-Ezike, Enugu State, Nigeria, November 1996.

In 1922, King Ahebi took advantage of the power and authority of her office to use forced labor to build the Ahebi Ugbabe Road. In 1930, Ahebi set up a school in her palace, but attendance was extremely poor. The teacher, in an attempt to boost enrollment, introduced himself to the elders of Enugu-Ezike. He was told that the school should not be in Ahebi's palace, but in the oldest man's house, according to tradition. The teacher, therefore, moved into the oldest man's house. A slighted Ahebi called in the police, who rounded up all the elders involved and threw them into Nsukka prison for three days.

The underlying reason that the elders encouraged the teacher to move out of Ahebi's palace was that they had had enough of her antics and abuses. It was not enough that Ahebi had eroded the traditional leadership of male elders and abused her political power. The final straw was when she created and brought out a masked spirit. This single act shook the fabric of the society to the point that the case had to be taken to the Resident's Office in Onitsha. The resident was the highest court of the time. After the resident heard the case, he informed Ahebi that she did not have a right to create a masquerade because she was a woman. He instructed the villagers to repay Ahebi whatever money she had used to acquire the masked spirit, and then keep the masquerade.

This decision of the court revealed the duplicity of the British colonials. Their relationship with Ahebi was almost entirely unilateral. They had used Ahebi's knowledge of the geography of her town to conquer and subjugate her people. Then they patted her on the back by granting her a warrant chief position. They had superficially supported her during conflicts in her community, but when it really counted, they betrayed her in the worst possible way.

As soon as the resident instructed Ahebi to relinquish her masquerade to the community, her influence lessened, and her image as superhuman and untouchable unraveled. Ahebi would become marginalized and somewhat ostracized; in the end, she was forced to perform her own burial rites while living (i.e., *ikwa onwe ya na ndu*) for she feared that no one in her community would grant her a befitting burial.[10]

Paramount Chief Mosadi Seboko

Born on June 7, 1950, in Ramotswa, a town south of Gaborone, Mosadi Seboko was the first woman to become *kgosikgolo* (paramount chief) of the Balete people of Botswana. Her name, Mosadi, means "woman," and she was so named by a dissatisfied father who had hoped that he would have a son. She attended Moeding College, graduating in 1969, and became a department administrator at Barclay's Bank two years later. In 1978, she ended a six-year marriage to an abusive husband.

When her father, Chief Kgosi Mokgosi I, died, her uncle ruled as regent in place of her young brother, Kgosi Seboko II. After her uncle died in 1996, her brother succeeded him as kgosikgolo. In 2001, Kgosi Seboko II died without an heir. Mosadi and her brother's paternal uncles chose a male cousin to succeed him. Mosadi Seboko was not considered a viable heir or kgosi because she was a woman. The office of kgosikgolo was traditionally reserved for men; women could only serve as regents. Mosadi, however, challenged the appointment of her male cousin, claiming that her being passed over solely because she was female was discriminatory. Mosadi's mother and six sisters threw their support behind her, and her uncles grudgingly sanctioned her assuming the office of regent, but not paramount chief.

As a consequence, Mosadi served as regent for about a year, after which she again took up the fight to be appointed paramount chief, a station that she argued was her birthright (*bogosi*), given that she was the first born.

In the face of her uncles' disapproval, Mosadi cited the Botswanan constitution, which disavows discrimination on the basis of gender or sex. In this fight, she garnered the support of Botswanan women involved in the women's rights movement. In December 2001, hundreds of Balete people and members of the royal family assembled at the royal court to discuss Mosadi Seboko's quest for the chieftaincy. Despite protests from members who wanted to uphold so-called tradition, the royal court decided in her favor, allowing her to become the first female paramount chief of the Balete people of Botswana. Mosadi officially took up her position as paramount chief on January 7, 2002, and has remained a powerful and influential leader.[11]

African women who have ruled as men were able to assume leadership positions as gendered males because of the flexibility and fluidity of the African gender construct, which allows women to become gendered men and men, gendered women. These masculine (wo)men lead from male spaces, often projecting masculine-centered leadership values, and occupying (as much as possible) spaces that were constructed by society as quintessentially male.

In chapter 5, I explore the roles of educated African women in postcolonial and national politics, economics, and religion today, allowing me to bring my exploration of the political, economic, and religious worlds of African women full circle. From presidents to parliamentarians, business women to tech giants, prophetesses to women evangelical leaders, and everything in between, African women have had to contend with the disastrous impact of colonialism on their lives and structures of power. The consequence is that they are still recovering from the disadvantaged position they found themselves under colonialism and have not yet been able to realize their full precolonial potential. It is how the educated political, economic, and religious elite are propelling their lives forward in these three realms that is the focus of the next chapter.

African Women Today

In this chapter, I explore African women's power, influence, and authority in three important spheres of political, religious, and economic endeavor today. While African women have served as female monarchs—both human and spiritual—and merchant queens since ancient times, colonial, missionary, and Islamic encroachments have disrupted and undermined African women's and the female spiritual principle's political, religious, and economic autonomy; the postcolonial era nevertheless marked a period of renewal, of revitalization, in which African women have struggled to achieve a semblance of the independence, power, authority, and influence that they had pre-contact. Each woman chronicled in this chapter has reached the pinnacle of her chosen profession. She is, simply put, a member of the political, religious, and economic elite. She is powerful, she is influential, and she wields considerable authority at the highest levels. The common denominator that connects the reflections in this fifth chapter and sets it apart from my discussions, in the four preceding chapters, of women's precolonial power and authority in the same domains is the fact that all the women presented in this chapter have completed the equivalent of a tertiary education.

Politics

Colonialism marked the beginning of the end of any kind of equality between African men and women in politics. During the postcolonial era, however, African women have sought to reestablish the political clout they lost during colonial encroachment. This challenge has been met with varying degrees of success. The postcolonial era has seen the emergence of select African women occupying office at the highest levels of national government. They have governed as heads of state—the highest executive legal authority of their nations—either as presidents or as prime ministers. They have been world leaders. Some have been appointed on an interim or acting basis; others have been elected. Still others have served their countries as vice presidents, members of parliament, and ministers. This section concerns itself with African women politicians who fill positions of high office at the national level.

Presidents, Prime Ministers, and Vice Presidents

The Central African Republic was the first country in Africa to have a woman head of state. Elisabeth Domitien became prime minister on January 2, 1975, and remained in office for a year and three months. After she stepped down, it would take the better part of a decade—until the mid-1980s—for Africa to field another female head of government.

The mid-1980s and the 1990s would usher in an era of renewed political activism among women across Africa. During these decades, women in five African countries—Tanzania, Angola, Central African Republic, Guinea-Bissau, and Nigeria—ran for office as presidential candidates.

Born in the city of Bissau, Portuguese Guinea, in 1937, Carmen Pereira was elected president of the Guinea-Bissau People's National Assembly in 1984, a decade after the country achieved independence, and while holding that post was appointed acting president of Guinea-Bissau for three days, May 14–16, 1984, as the country's new constitution was ratified. She was thus the first African woman to serve as president of an independent nation. Before that, she had served as deputy president of the assembly from 1973 to 1984. Between 1975 and 1980, she was also president of the Cape Verde Parliament (at that time, Cape Verde was united with Guinea-Bissau), and from 1981 to 1983, Pereira served as minister of health and social affairs in Guinea-Bissau. After leaving the National Assembly in 1989 to join the Council of State, she briefly held the posts of minister of state for social affairs and deputy prime minister before being dismissed by President João Bernardo Vieira in 1992. President Pereira passed away on June 16, 2016, after an illustrious political career.

On July 10, 1993, in the eastern part of the continent, Sylvie Kinigi (b. 1953) was sworn in as prime minister of Burundi, becoming acting president about three months later when President Melchior Ndadaye was killed by Tutsi rebels. She was the first woman to hold either post, serving until February 1994. Eight days after Sylvie Kinigi became prime minister of Burundi, Agathe Uwilingiyimana was sworn in as prime minister of Burundi's troubled neighbor, Rwanda. A few months later, on the evening of April 6, 1994, a plane carrying the president of Rwanda—Juvénal Habyarimana, a moderate Hutu—and President Cyprien Ntaryamira of Burundi was shot down, killing everyone on board. Hutu extremists were blamed. The next day, Prime Minister Uwilingiyimana, also a moderate Hutu, was assassinated. This was the beginning of the organized and systematic killing of Tutsi and moderate Hutu. Uwilingiyimana's murder was part of a campaign to exterminate moderate Hutu or Tutsi politicians, with the aim of forming an interim government of Hutu extremists with Colonel Théoneste Bagosora at the helm.

The east African nation of Uganda had the first female vice president on the continent—Dr. Wandira Kazibwe, born in 1954 and educated at the Makerere University School of Medicine, who held that office between 1994 and 2003. Other African nations that have had female vice presidents are The Gambia (Isatou Njie-Saidy, 1997–2017, and Fatoumata Jallow Tambajang, 2017–18), Malawi (Joyce Banda, 2009–12), Tanzania (Samia Suluhu, 2015–), and Zambia (Inonge Mutukwa Wina, 2015–).

On September 3, 1996, Ruth Perry was appointed chairperson of the Council of State for Liberia. This appointment was equivalent to the head of state and government. She held the position for a little less than a year. Then there was Mame Madior Boye, who became the prime minister of Senegal on March 3, 2001, and Prime Minister Maria das Neves of São Tomé and Príncipe, who held office from October 3, 2002, to September 18, 2004.

Also in 2004, Luisa Diogo (b. 1958) became prime minister of Mozambique, a position she held until January 2010. Born in the western Mozambique province of Tete, she studied economics at Maputo's Eduardo Mondlane University. She would serve as Mozambique's minister of finance from 1999 until 2004. Named one of *Time* magazine's top leaders and revolutionaries in the world, Diogo was a progressive reformer, passionate advocate for women's empowerment, and savvy businesswoman.

In 2005, Maria do Carmo Silveira was elected prime minister of São Tomé and Príncipe, a position that she held for almost a year. The next January (2006), Ellen Johnson-Sirleaf became the first elected African female president, and the twenty-fourth president of Liberia. She concluded her term as president of that war-torn country in 2018.

Ivy Matsepe-Casaburri of South Africa holds the record for being the shortest-serving acting president of an African country. She held the position for fourteen hours from September 24 to September 25, 2008. Cécile

Manorohanta, acting prime minister of Madagascar, did not last much longer; she occupied the position for two days in December 2009.

On the west coast of the continent, Rose Francine Rogombé was appointed acting president of Gabon, a position she held for 128 days in 2009. In Mali, Cissé Mariam Kaïdama Sidibé became prime minister and head of government on April 3, 2011, and was removed from office in a military coup March 22, 2012. For sixty-two days between February and April 2012, Adiato Djaló Nandigna of Guinea-Bissau was the acting prime minister. In Africa's third-smallest country, Mauritius, Monique Ohsan Bellepeau, the country's first female vice president, was acting president from March to July 2012 and again briefly in 2015.

Malawi's female president, Joyce Hilda Banda, was sworn in on April 7, 2012, following the sudden death of President Bingu wa Mutharika. Aminata Touré of Senegal became prime minister and head of government on September 1, 2013, and held the post until July 8, 2014. Then there was Catherine Samba-Panza, acting president of the Central African Republic, who was head of state from January 23, 2014, to March 30, 2016. Saara Kuugongelwa of Namibia is the incumbent prime minister of Namibia.

Sworn in June 2015, Ameenah Gurib-Fakim (b. 1959) was president and commander-in-chief of Mauritius. A leading biodiversity scientist, Ameenah Gurib-Fakim evaluated the flora of Mauritius for its health, nutritional, and cosmetic functions prior to becoming president. Ameenah Gurib-Fakim also held an endowed chair at the University of Mauritius as professor of organic chemistry. She was an entrepreneur and managing director of the Centre International de Développement Pharmaceutique (CIDP) Research and Innovation. She would remain president until she was asked to step down on March 9, 2018, after a scandal over expenses. On March 14, 2018, she announced that she had not in fact stepped down; she intimated that she was being forced out for what amounted to a misunderstanding over monies ($13,000) that she had already paid back in full. On March 23, 2018, she was finally forced out of office.[1]

Sahle-Work Zewde (b. 1950), president of the Federal Democratic Republic of Ethiopia, is Africa's newest, and only current, woman president. She is also Ethiopia's first female president. The married mother of two sons was born in Addis Ababa to a father who was a senior officer in the imperial army. On October 25, 2018, she was unanimously elected president by the Federal Parliamentary Assembly. A multilingual career diplomat, she is fluent in Amhara, French, and English, and has served in Senegal, Cape Verde, Guinea-Bissau, The Gambia, Guinea-Conakry, and France. She also previously served as special representative of the United Nations to the African Union.

Her election as president came a week after Ethiopian prime minister Abiy Ahmed Ali overhauled his

Figure 5.1. Sahle-Work Zewde at the United Nations Office in Nairobi, 2016. Photograph by J. Marchand, September 5, 2016.

cabinet. He reduced the number of cabinet ministers from twenty-eight to twenty and then named women to half of the ministerial positions in his cabinet. Significantly, the prime minister named women to the two most prominent cabinet offices: minister of defense and the newly created minister of peace, who oversees intelligence and security forces.[2]

The Parliament and National Legislature

The twenty-first century ushered in gains for African women in other arenas of national politics, with women averaging 23.7 percent of parliamentary seats in sub-Saharan Africa. Twenty-six African countries currently rank in the top 100 worldwide for women representation in their national legislatures or parliaments. In October 2003, Rwanda came closer than any national legislature in the world at the time to reaching parity between men and women. By September 2008, the country surpassed parity, with 56.3 percent of seats held by women, and as of early 2020 Rwanda still ranked first in the world, with 61.25 percent of seats in the lower house held by women, far outstripping no. 2, Cuba. With women elected to 46.43 percent of its parliamentary seats, South Africa ranks tenth in the world in the number of women members of a legislature, followed among African countries by Senegal (14th, 43.03 percent), Namibia (15th, 42.71 percent), Mozambique (18th, 41.2 percent), Ethiopia (29th, 38.76 percent), Tanzania (34th, 36.9 percent), Burundi (35th, 36.36 percent), Uganda (37th, 34.86 percent), Guyana (38th, 34.78 percent), Zimbabwe (45th, 31.85 percent), and Cameroon (49th, 31.11 percent). Other African nations in the top 100 for women representation in 2020 are Angola (52nd), South Sudan (61st), Algeria (72nd), Cabo Verde (73rd), Tunisia (76th), Somalia (78th), Lesotho (the third-smallest—and landlocked—country

in mainland Africa, tied with Israel at 83rd, and trailing
the United States by only a tenth of a percentage point),
Malawi (85th), Guinea (86th), Kenya (92nd), Seychelles
(94th), and Equatorial Guinea (97th).[3]

Women Ministers

Ministers are politicians who hold public office in
national or regional governments. They make and im-
plement decisions on national and regional policies. In
some countries, the head of government is also a minister and is designated prime minister (see discussion
above). In this section, I present material on women
ministers in a cross-section of Africa countries serving at the national level. As you will see, the majority
of these women serve in the important and powerful
role of foreign minister, which is the equivalent of the
United States' secretary of state.

One of the earliest female ministers in Africa was
Egyptian. Appointed in 1962, Hikmat Abu Zayd was
the minister for social affairs. Eight years later in the
Central African Republic, Marie-Josephe Franck was
appointed government minister. In Uganda, Princess
Elizabeth Bagaya of Toro was made foreign minister in
1974. A year later, in Mauritania, Aïssata Kane was made
government minister. It would take until 2009 for an-
other minister, this time Foreign Minister Naha Mint
Mouknass, to be appointed in Mauritania. In 1978, in
São Tomé and Príncipe, Maria do Nascimento da Graça
Amorim was appointed foreign minister and Maria das

Neves became prime minister in 2002. The next year, Gloria Amon Nikoi of Ghana was made foreign minister.

Between 1982 and 2020, the country of Algeria had twenty-three female federal government ministers who occupied important offices. Zuhur Wanasi was the first woman to hold high governmental office in Algeria. She was minister of social affairs in 1982, and minister for social protection in 1984. Several women ministers were appointed in the election year of 2014, including Nadia Labidi, minister of culture; Nouria Benghabrit-Remaoun, minister of education; Dalila Boudjemaa, minister of land-use planning and environment; Mounia Meslem, minister of family and women; Zahra Dardouri, minister of post, information technology, and communication; Nouria Yamina Zerhouni, minister of tourism; and Aish Tabagho, minister of art and handicrafts. In 2015, Houda-Imane Faraoun was appointed minister of post, information technology, and communication. In 2017, Algeria had three female ministers: Houda-Imane Feraoun; Ghania Eddalia, minister of national solidarity, family, and the status of women; and Fatma-Zohra Zerouati, minister of the environment and renewable energy. Algeria's newly constituted 2020 cabinet has five women ministers.[4]

Between 1983 and 2014, Algeria's neighbor, Tunisia, appointed women to eight ministerial positions, including Fethia Mzali, minister of women's affairs (1983); Souad Yaacoubi, minister of public health (1984); Faïza Kefi, minister of the environment (1999) and minister of vocational training (2001); Neziha Zarrouk, minister of employment (2001); Moufida Tlatli, minister of culture (2011); Nejla Moalla, minister of commerce (2014); and Amel Karboul, minister of tourism (2014).

In the Democratic Republic of Congo, Ekila Liyonda was appointed foreign minister in 1987. Two years later, Rina Venter was appointed health minister in South Africa. Then in 1999, Nkosazana Dlamini-Zuma was made foreign minister. In the Seychelles, Danielle de St. Jorre was made foreign minister. Her appointment took effect in 1989. Two years later in the West African nation of Gabon, Pascaline Mferri Bongo was appointed foreign minister.

In Liberia, Dorothy Musuleng-Cooper was made foreign minister in 1994. In the same year, Sy Kadiatou Sow was made foreign minister in Mali. In 1995, two ministers were appointed in Mauritius: Marie Claude Arouff-Parfait, who was made minister of youth and sports; and Indira Thacoor Sidaya, who was made minister of gender equality, child development, and family welfare. In 2005, Sheila Bappoo was made minister of social security, national solidarity, and reform institutions in the same country; and in 2014, Leela Devi Dookhun Luchoomun was made Mauritius's minister of education and human resources.

In 1996, Shirley Gbujama was made foreign minister of Sierra Leone. Two years later, Lila Ratsifandrihamanana became Madagascar's foreign minister. Aïchatou Mindaoudou was also made foreign minister in 1999 in the Republic of Niger. In 2000 and 2005, Lilian Patel was made foreign minister and Anna Kachikho, interior minister. Cecile Manorohanta was made Niger's defense minister in 2007. Guinea-Bissau has had as many as three female federal ministers, including Hilia Barber, who was made foreign minister in 1999, and Filomenda Mascarenhas Tipote, made defense minister in 2005.

In 2000, Mahawa Bangoura became the first female foreign minister of the Republic of Guinea, followed two years later, in Cape Verde, by Fatima Veiga. Africa's most populous nation, Nigeria, has had a slew of female ministers, including Ngozi Okonjo-Iweala, who became finance minister in 2003 and again in 2006. In 2003, Edna Adan Ismail was made foreign minister of Somaliland. Two years later, in 2005, Mozambique appointed Alcinda Abreu foreign minister. That same year, Rosalia Nghidinwa was appointed Namibia's interior minister, followed in 2013 by Netumbo Nandi-Ndaitwah, who was made foreign minister.

In 2006, two more women were appointed foreign minister: Asha-Rose Migiro in Tanzania and Mariam Aladji Boni Diallo in Benin. In 2007, Morocco appointed five female federal government ministers: Amina Benkhadra, minister of energy and mines; Nawal El Moutawakel, minister of sports; Nouzha Skalli, minister of solidarity, women, family, and social development; Touriya Jabrane, minister of culture; and Yasmina Baddou, minister of health. Six years later,

Bassima Hakkaoui was appointed minister of solidarity, women, family, and social development.

In 2008, Rosemary Museminali was appointed the Rwandan minister of foreign affairs. In Kenya, Martha Karua was made minister of constitutional affairs in 2008 and Amina Mohamed became foreign minister in 2013. In Libya, in 2011 Fatima Hamroush was made minister of health. Zambia appointed two female ministers, in 2011 and 2012: Inonge Wina was made minister of chiefs and traditional affairs, and Inonge Wina was made minister of gender and child development. Susan Waffa-Ogoo (Gambia) and Fowsiyo Yusuf Haji Adan (Somalia) were appointed foreign ministers in 2012. Finally, Leonie Banga-Bothy was made foreign minister of the Central African Republic in 2013.[5] The year 2018 saw the appointment of ten women ministers in Ethiopia, making women 50 percent of the cabinet of Africa's second-most populous nation. Moreover, these women leaders are in charge of some of the most important ministries in the country including defense and security, trade, transport, and labor, as well as culture, science, and revenue.[6]

What was it about the 1990s and afterward that allowed African women to make these political advances? Political scientists Aili Tripp, Dior Konaté, and Colleen Lowe-Morna offer the following circumstances in explanation: (a) the move toward multipartism in most African countries; (b) the fact that women's movements were increasingly geared toward political leadership and reform movements; (c) the development of quota systems in Africa that were designed to rectify gender gaps, especially in countries like Senegal, Namibia, South Africa, and Tunisia; (d) the effect of the international women's movement, especially the Beijing Conference on Women in 1995. All these factors, they suggest, gave African women the added zeal to agitate for positive political change—changes that moved them closer to their precolonial reality.[7]

Religion

How are women faring as religious leaders today? Although U.S. Department of State statistics on practitioners of indigenous African religions in Africa range from a low of about 1 percent (São Tomé and Príncipe) to a high of 52 percent (Madagascar),[8] these numbers grossly underestimate women's participation.[9] Indigenous African religions operate side by side with Christianity and Islam, exuding particular vibrancy in the rural areas. However, because this chapter is about African women who have been educated in the Western and/or Islamic tradition beyond the tertiary level, we will not concern ourselves with the multiplicity of leadership experiences of African women/female principle in indigenous African religions—an engagement that has found expression in some of the preceding chapters (see especially chapter 1). This chapter instead takes its bearing from the postindependence periods, which witnessed African women working to regain some of their precolonial religious authority, which had been eroded by the impact of Islam and Christianity. The 1990s and beyond would usher in religious politicking by African women, who increasingly demanded prominence not only within the Christian churches—whose parishioners were mostly female—but also under Islam. The African Church movement, or Ethiopianism, would find a renewed expression in nations as varied as Nigeria, South Africa, Rwanda, South Sudan, and Kenya. In the sections that follow, I discuss African women who have occupied leadership positions at the highest ranks in the Christian church movement.

Abimbola Rosemary Bimbo Odukoya (1960–2005) was a Nigerian pastor, televangelist, conference speaker, youth mentor, marriage counselor, and writer. Odukoya received a Bachelor of Arts degree in history and archaeology from the University of Ibadan. Between 1987 and 1999, she worked at the Redeemed Evangelical Mission as the head of counseling. Shortly after that, she married Pastor Taiwo Odukoya, founder of the Fountain of Life Church; they have three children. Bimbo Odukoya published four books, including *Marriage: Real People, Real Problems, Wise Counsel;* and *Living Free: Overcoming Masturbation.* She received over sixty national and international awards for her work. She was the host of *Single and Married,* a nationally and internationally televised program that explored issues that individuals faced in marriages and relationships. Bimbo Odukoya died December 11, 2005, in a plane crash in Port

Harcourt, Nigeria. At the time of her death, she was the associate senior pastor of the Fountain of Life Church and president of Discovery for Women.[10]

Pastor Faith Abiola Oyedepo is senior pastor of Faith Tabernacle, Canaanland, Ota, Nigeria. She has spent over three decades preaching the word of God, with a mission to feed the poor, liberate the oppressed, and care for the sick. She is vice president of the Education Department of the Living Faith Church Worldwide, and the proprietor of Covenant University. She has written twenty-six books, which include *Guidelines to Effective Personal Bible Study, Making Marriage Work, Understanding Motherhood,* and *Raising Godly Children.* Her books explore marital issues and the individual's relationship with God.[11]

Regarded as the mother of the Agape Christian Ministries, the church that she and her husband founded, Funke Felix-Adejumo (an accomplished pastor and teacher) is also the president of Funke Felix-Adejumo Foundation, which is committed to women's empowerment. Her passion to better the lives of Nigerian women and children has informed the projects that she has undertaken, including establishing the Grace Orphanage and the Children's Hospital. A sought-after speaker, Adejumo has published over fifty well-received books, including *If Not for God! Fifty Lessons Life Taught Me, My Seed Is Designed for the Palace,* and *Mothers' Summit Prayer Points.*[12] Another Nigerian reverend, Funke Adetuberu, runs the Women College of Ministry, which has graduated hundreds of women. She has also published forty-two books.[13]

Nigeria's neighbor Ghana has also produced a number of prominent women pastors. Reverend Adelaide Heward-Mills, for instance, has been involved in Christian ministry for over twenty years. She serves as executive director of the Daughter You Can Make It Ministry. A prolific preacher, she has numerous gospel podcasts addressing issues pertaining to intimacy with God, love, relationships, marriage, and womanhood.[14]

At least two southern African women bishops have achieved prominence in their churches. The first, Ellinah Ntombi Wamukoya, is an Anglican bishop of her Eswatini dioceses, the first woman to be elected bishop of the Anglican Church in Africa. Elected by a two-thirds majority of the Elective Assembly on July 18, 2012, Bishop Wamukoya was consecrated on November 17, 2012, by Archbishop Thabo Makgoba. Wamukoya studied at the universities of Botswana, Lesotho, and Eswatini. She previously served as chaplain of the University of Eswatini and St. Michael's High School in Manzini. Bishop Wamukoya's successes in ministry paved the way for the election of a second African woman bishop, Margaret Vertue.[15] A diocesan bishop of the Anglican Diocese of False Bay, South Africa, Vertue was educated at St. Paul's Theological College, Grahamstown, Stellenbosch University, and St. Beuno's in North Wales. In September 1992, she was ordained as one of Africa's first women priests by Archbishop Desmond

Tutu. She was elected bishop of False Bay on October 3, 2012, and was consecrated on January 19, 2013, by the Most Reverend Thabo Makgoba, archbishop of Cape Town.[16]

In the Horn of Africa, Elizabeth Awut Ngor was consecrated Anglican bishop of South Sudan on December 31, 2016. Hers was a controversial consecration, because she was the first woman to become a bishop in a province of the Anglican Communion that aligns itself with the Global Anglican Future Conference (GAFCON), a conservative Anglican movement that disapproves of homosexuality and supports limiting women's leadership roles and ordination in the Anglican communion. In a 2014 meeting of GAFCON primates, they agreed not to consecrate women as bishops until a task force was set up to offer recommendations. Thus, the Task Force on Women in the Episcopate was established in April 2015; two years later the task force upheld the 2014 recommendation to only consecrate men as bishops. Even so, Elizabeth Awut Ngor's position as bishop in South Sudan stands in marked contrast to the status quo.[17]

In Kenya, Kathy Kiuna and Teresia Wairimu serve as reverends of important churches. Kathy Kiuna is a worship leader, associate pastor, and singer at Jubilee Christian Church, Parklands, Nairobi. She cohosts a weekly television program, *Voice of Jubilee,* with her husband, Bishop Allan Kiuna. Like many African women Christian leaders, Reverend Kiuna directs her ministry toward women. Working with the Daughters of Zion Ladies Ministry, she ministers to thousands of women, offering a helping hand to those in need, as well as to those who have suffered abuse. Kathy Kiuna is also an accomplished singer and worship leader who has released three Christian music albums.[18]

A founder and director of Faith Evangelistic Ministry, Reverend Teresia Wairimu was born in 1957. Almost thirty years later, in 1985, she was called to serve God. Her fellowship started small. Her congregants first assembled in a house, then moved to a city hall, and now, she and her congregants worship at Kenyatta International Conference Centre, one of the largest auditoriums in Nairobi. Prominent political figures such as William Ruto, deputy president in the Uhuru government, worship at Reverend Wairimu's church. Today, Reverend Wairimu is unquestionably one of the most influential religious leaders in Kenya.[19]

With approximately 44 percent of the African population being Muslim, accounting for a quarter of the world's Muslim population,[20] African Islamic women leaders today do not feature nearly as centrally in the leadership of their mosques and religious communities as Christian women do. They have nevertheless organized themselves into action groups[21] that agitate for gendered representation and change in all aspects of Muslim women's lives, especially under Sharia law. These groups, located in the Horn and East Africa (Tanzania, Eritrea, Ethiopia, Somalia, and the Sudan), South

Africa, and West Africa (Nigeria, Ghana, Mauritania, Burkina Faso, Chad, Cameroon, Mali, Niger, and Senegal), tackle issues involving women's rights to control their bodies (particularly in respect to circumcision in its various forms), inheritance and custody rights, and rights to educational resources. All of this illuminates the fact that African Muslim women, regardless of obstacles, are active participants in the making of their own histories.

Some Muslim women in Africa, despite popular perception, have excelled as educators, scholars, poets, and activists. One of the most prominent female Muslim scholars was Nana Asma'u bint Shehu Uthman dan Fodio (a.k.a. Nana Asma'u; 1793–1864) of the Sokoto Caliphate, the seat of which is in what is now northern Nigeria. Born to the religious leader Uthman dan Fodio, Asma'u gained prominence as a female community leader who organized and resocialized enslaved people and refugees, especially women in the Caliphate. She was a proponent of women's education and independence under Islam, and she and her work are viewed by many as the predecessor to modern Islamic feminism in Africa. She was also a prolific and fine poet, who published over five dozen poems of guidance, including elegies, laments, and admonitions. Her poems expand upon her father's teachings about the importance of women leaders and women's rights in Islam.[22]

In the Horn of Africa lived the distinguished Muslim poet and scholar Mana Sitti Habib Jamaladdin (ca.

1810s–1919), affectionately called Dada Masiti (grand-mother Masiti). Born in Brava, southern Somalia, to the Ashraf family, which traced its descent from the Prophet Mohammed, the teenage Mana Sitti Habib Jamaladdin was kidnapped and held in Zanzibar in slave-like conditions for ten years. She escaped and was rescued by her maternal uncle, Omar Qullatten. Upon her return to Brava, Mana Sitti Habib Jamaladdin devoted herself to religious studies under the guidance of Sheikh Mohammed Janna al-Bahluli. She attained a high level of proficiency, becoming a shining example of holiness, such that she commanded the respect and admiration of all learned Muslim men of her generation. Dada Masti lived to be over 100 years old, celebrated for her emotionally eloquent and imaginative poetry. Her poems were memorized and transmitted from one Bravanese generation to the next. Muslim poets extolled her piety and noble lineage in verse, praising her mastery of the poetic form. One noted poet, Sheikh Qasim Muhyiddin al-Barawi, celebrated her in verse thus: "Dada Masiti, pray for me" he wrote, further intimating that love for Masiti "is the foundation of all true faith."[23]

In recent years, some African Muslim women have, contrary to the norm, served as prayer leaders (*imams*), leading their congregations in *salat* (prayer). In South Africa, some of these Muslim women include Dr. Lubna Nadvi, Zaytun, Suleyman, Fatima Seedat, Fatima Hendricks, Dr. Mariam Seedat, and Zulaykha Maya.[24]

In Morocco, Khadija al-Aktam, Samera Masouk, and Zireb Hidra are *mourchidats* (female Muslim clerics). The word *mourchidat* means "female guide," and the expressed role of these female clerics is to help introduce and lead a more moderate Islam in Morocco. They are expected to help Muslim Moroccan women with religious questions and their education and to provide support for them in schools and prisons. This Moroccan government initiative was part of a wave of liberal reform begun by King Mohammed VI in 2004. These mourchidats first made news in April 2006 when the Moroccan government announced that the first fifty female clerics had graduated from the Dar al-Hadith al-Hassania seminary.

To be granted a spot in the seminary to study to become a mourchidat, each woman had to pass an entrance exam and interview. She also had to have a bachelor's degree. These female candidates were required to live a life grounded in the Qur'an, meaning that each had to have memorized it and showed an understanding of *tajwid* (the art of Qur'anic recital). Once at the seminary, the women studied psychology, sociology, computer science, economics, law, and business management. They also trained in Islamic studies, taking as much as three hours of homework home every day. On graduation, each mourchidat is assigned a mosque, and there is special attention to finding one close to their families. Once assigned, the mourchidat offers women spiritual advice and teaches them the Qur'an. They also discuss more

Figure 5.2. Quran, Mus'haf Al Tajweed. Photograph by Amr Fayez (TheEgyptian), undated.

contentious gender-related issues such as sex, women's health, and what to do if your husband beats you— matters that women would not feel comfortable discussing with a male imam.

Samera Masouk (b. 1976) serves as mourchidat in Rabat, Morocco. A leader of one of the area's more than three hundred mosques, Masouk works twelve-hour days in her assigned mosque and has responsibility for sixty-seven other mosques in Rabat. As a mourchidat, she consults with children in nearby schools and women in hospitals, runs activities for two hundred women prisoners, and supports many ex-prisoners once they are released. Another mourchidat, Zireb Hidra (b. 1967), works in an east Casablanca mosque. Her power is evident in the number of women who line the stairs leading up to the mosque. They also line the homes close to the mosque and spill out of the doors and windows. At a given time, there are as many as one hundred women and children who come to her to seek advice, which speaks to her popularity and influence.[25]

Shamima Shaikh (1960–1998) was a notable Islamic feminist and journalist in South Africa. She was South Africa's best-known Muslim women's rights activist. Born in Louis Trichardt, Limpopo Province, Shaikh studied at the University of Durban-Westville, completing her bachelor's degree in Arabic and psychology in 1984. While there, she became involved in the Azanian People's Organization (AZAPO).

In 1989, Shaikh worked for the Muslim community newspaper, *al-Qalam*. She also became involved in the Muslim Youth Movement of South Africa (MYM). Between 1993 and 1996, she served as the first national coordinator of the Muslim Youth Movement Gender Desk. With Shaikh at the helm, the MYM Gender Desk became the most outspoken Muslim organization fighting for Muslim women's rights and articulating Islamic feminism. As Gender Desk coordinator, she organized workshops, seminars, and campaigns, including MYM's "Campaign for a Just Muslim Personal Law" and "Equal Access to Mosques."

Shaikh was also involved in a coalition of Muslim bodies that organized the Muslim Forum on Elections and called for a vote in South Africa's first democratic elections in April 1994, in particular, to support parties like the African National Congress (ANC) and the Pan Africanist Congress (PAC), which had been involved in the liberation movement.

In 1994, Shaikh became the first chairperson of the Muslim Community Broadcasting Trust. She also founded the Muslim Personal Law Board of South Africa. In the same year, while battling breast cancer, she was appointed managing editor of *al-Qalam*, which, under her leadership, became the flagship journal of progressive expression of Islam in South Africa. In August 1997, she launched the Muslim community radio station, "The Voice." She would succumb to breast cancer on January 8, 1998.[26]

Economics

How are African women faring in the economic realm of their societies today? Although the exceptionally important role of women as economic producers in their societies (see chapter 3) was overlooked by the colonial governments in favor of African men, in the present day African women remain the backbone of economic growth on the continent. According to a 2018 report of the MasterCard Index of Women's Entrepreneurship (MIWE), Africa has the highest growth rate of women entrepreneurs. Moreover, African women entrepreneurs have fared better than their European counterparts. For example, in Switzerland one out of every four companies is owned by women, whereas in Ghana women own one-half of the companies. In fact, Ghana has the highest percentage of women business owners worldwide. And Uganda comes in third overall.

More than half of all African women work independently, running microbusinesses as diverse as market stands, "mama put" restaurants, and small boutiques. Most of these entrepreneurs, the majority of whom are uneducated, are driven by grit and determination along with the desire to earn enough to keep themselves and their extended families afloat.[27] Few achieve as much as the nouveau riche women entrepreneurs of Africa. This new crop of millionaires and billionaires are either self-made, inheritance-trust, or corruption-enabled entrepreneurs who have distinguished themselves in business at the highest levels in different parts of the continent. These are their stories.

With an estimated net worth of $3.3 billion, Angolan investor and businesswoman Isabel dos Santos is Africa's richest woman and one of the continent's most powerful and influential businesswomen. She is the eldest daughter of Angolan president José Eduardo dos Santos, who held that office from 1979 to 2017. Isabel accumulated her wealth in oil, diamonds, communications, and banking. Appointed by her father in June 2016 as head of Sonangol, Angola's state oil firm, she would be removed from that role by Angola's new president in November 2017. She boasts shareholdings in Portuguese banks and energy firms such as Banco Portugues de Investimento and Portuguese Energias de Portugal. In early 2020, she continued to serve as chairwoman

Figure 5.3. Isabel dos Santos. Photograph by Nuno Coimbra, January 28, 2019.

of Unitel SA—one of Angola's largest mobile network companies, valued at more than $5 billion—amid allegations of corruption. She presently lives in exile in the UAE, but is facing prosecution in her home country of Angola for corruption crimes, with the Angolan government freezing her bank accounts and confiscating her assets in Angola, Portugal, and elsewhere.[28]

Nigeria's Folorunsho Alakija is Africa's second-richest woman. Her entry into business was at the helm of a fashion company, whose label dressed the Nigerian elite, including the then first lady of Nigeria, Mrs. Mariam

178

Babangida. She later became vice chair of Famfa Oil, a Nigerian oil exploration company, with an abundant offshore field called Agbami. In 1993, the Nigerian government awarded Famfa Oil an oil prospecting license, and a few years later, an oil mining lease. The Agbami field has been operating since 2008 and Famfa Oil's partners include Chevron and Petrobras.[29]

When South African–born Sibongile Sambo applied for a flight attendant job with South African Airways, she was rejected because she did not meet the minimum height requirement. Instead of giving up her dream, she started her own aviation business. Today, she is the founder and managing director of SRS Aviation, the first black female-owned aviation company in South Africa. Another South African businesswoman, Bridgette Radebe, began her career as a contract miner, who managed shafts in the 1980s. Several years later, she would become South Africa's first black female mining entrepreneur and president of the country's largest mining chamber, the South African Mining Development Association. Her company, Mmakau Mining, is a successful production company with interests in gold, platinum, coal, ferrochrome, and uranium.[30]

Divine Ndhlukula of Zimbabwe is another southern African woman who tackled a male-dominated industry head on: this time, the security and protection industry. In the late 1990s, she established the security company SECURICO in her cottage with four employees and very little capital. With more than 3,500 employees today,

SECURICO is one of the largest security firms in Zimbabwe. Starting with Mozambique and Zambia, Ndhlukula is set to expand her business into other countries on the continent. In 2017, Divine Ndhlukula was selected as one of the most influential women leaders in the world by Empowering a Billion Women by 2020, a global think tank, whose prior lists of influential women include world leaders and the likes of Michelle Obama, Hillary Clinton, and the former Mozambican first lady Graca Machel.[31]

Salwa Akhannouch of Morocco went into business in 1993 when she established a distribution company for flooring materials. Now one of Morocco's most prominent entrepreneurs, Salwa is the head of Akwa Group, a distribution company of petroleum products and the founder of Aksal Group, a Moroccan conglomerate specializing in luxury goods, retail, department stores, and shopping malls. Salwa holds the exclusive license to sell high-end fashion brands such as Zara, Gap, and Massimo Dutti in Morocco, and her company has a 50 percent stake in Morocco Mall, one of the largest shopping malls on the continent.[32]

Kenyan Tabitha Karanja is founding CEO of Keroche Breweries, the only large-scale brewery in Kenya owned by a Kenyan. Launched in 1997, the company initially manufactured fortified wine and spirits, and then starting in 2008, beer. Karanja's main beer brand, Summit, is so popular in the country that Karanja launched a $29 million expansion of Keroche Breweries in 2017. It is Karanja's plan to expand into the neighboring countries of Tanzania, Uganda, and Rwanda. Another Kenyan businesswoman, Njeri Rionge, started her first business at age nineteen, selling yogurt in Nairobi schools. She then made a transition into selling clothing and other small businesses. Today, Njeri Rionge is a pioneer investor in the IT sector in Africa. She is cofounder of Wananchi Online, East Africa's first and leading national internet service provider. Over the years, she has established several other thriving businesses, including the business consultancy Ignite Consulting; a health-care consultancy called Ignite Lifestyle; Business Lounge, one of Kenya's largest startup incubators; and Insite, a digital marketing agency.[33]

Finally, Bethlehem Tilahun Alemu grew up in a small underprivileged neighborhood in Addis Ababa. Although poor, most people living in her community possessed artisan skills. She sought to translate those skills into a business, and in 2004 soleRebels was born. An eco-friendly footwear company, and employer of hundreds of local talents, Alemu's company has grown to become one of the largest footwear companies in Africa, with flagship stores around the globe in countries like Taiwan, Spain, Switzerland, Austria, the United States, Singapore, and Japan. In 2011, the then thirty-six-year-old entrepreneur made the World Economic Forum's list of Young Global Leaders. She has also been named by *Forbes* magazine as one of Twenty Youngest Power Women in Africa, as well as one of the World's One Hundred Most Powerful Women.[34]

In this chapter, I consider the leadership roles that educated African women have occupied in the postcolonial era. This chapter brings the narratives of African women political, economic, and religious leaders to the present. It features the elite of the elite—women who have reached the pinnacle of their chosen fields and have served in the highest echelons of their national or federal governments, Christian and Islamic faiths, and business. What all women chronicled in this chapter have in common is that each is influential, exudes authority, and is powerful.

Conclusion

In *Female Monarchs and Merchant Queens in Africa,* I
have documented the lives and worlds of elite African women and females of privilege, highlighting the
similarities and differences in female leadership experience and potential in various geographical spaces and
settings. Whether they were leaders of their people or
wives of male leaders, these women of privilege exercised great power, authority, and influence publicly,
temporally, and in spiritual/religious spheres. From
centralized to small-scale egalitarian societies, patrilineal to matrilineal systems, North Africa to sub-Saharan
Africa, this book provides an overview of a representative group of remarkable African women and female
principles—seen and unseen—occupying positions of
power, authority, and influence.

Female Monarchs and Merchant Queens focuses
on the diverse forms of leadership, as well as on complexities of female power, at the highest level in various
African societies. I privilege an African-centered perspective that recognizes the existence of two distinct but
interconnected worlds and political constituencies—the

human and the spiritual—arguing that the gods and goddesses were the real rulers of African towns and human beings were merely there to interpret the will of the spirits. Thus, women leaders, including queens, queen mothers, princesses, merchant queens, and *female* kings are highlighted in my discussion of African women's leadership roles in the human political constituency. I document the leadership roles of spiritual monarchs (e.g., rain queens, spirit mediums, priestesses, goddesses, *sangomas,* female medicines, and prophetesses) in my discussion of the political constituency in the spiritual realm. The narrative throughout makes the connection between both African political constituencies. This text also highlights the economic and religious leadership roles that African women assumed in their precolonial societies. Conscious of the fact that these women found themselves occupying substantially diminished roles during the colonial era, which in many instances spilled over into the postcolonial era, *Female Monarchs and Merchant Queens in Africa* engages with African women's leadership realities in the postcolonial era, arguing that this era saw African women fight to evolve their roles into a semblance of their precolonial powerful expressions of political, economic, and religious power, authority, and influence. They did not always succeed, but this book features a cross section of some who did. These are *our* histories, *our* stories, *our* archives.

Notes

Introduction

1. Hamza Idris, "Women Arrest Boko Haram Fighters in Borno," *Daily Trust,* May 27, 2014, http://dailytrust.info /top-stories/25136-women-arrest-boko-haram-fighters-in -borno.

2. Founded in 2002 by Mohammed Yusuf of northern Nigeria, Boko Haram is a jihadist militant organization based in northern Nigeria but also active in Chad, Niger, and northern Cameroon.

3. Idris, "Women Arrest Boko Haram Fighters in Borno"; emphasis added.

4. Genderless Supreme Creator God of the Dogon people of West Africa.

5. Zulu goddess of agriculture.

6. Sobekneferu was the first known female ruler of Egypt.

7. Nzingha was a seventeenth-century female king of the Ndongo and Matamba Kingdoms of present-day Angola.

8. Nehanda, also known as Mbuya Nehanda, was a spirit medium of the Shona people of present-day Zimbabwe.

9. Ahebi Ugbabe was the only female king and warrant chief of British colonial Nigeria, and arguably, British Africa.

10. The *kandakes* of Meroë were sisters of the king or queen mothers of Kush in present-day Sudanese and southern Egyptian Nile Valley.

11. Omu Okwei was a merchant queen of Ossomari, Nigeria.

12. Nwando Achebe, *Farmers, Traders, Warriors, and Kings: Female Power and Authority in Northern Igboland, 1900–1960* (Portsmouth, NH: Heinemann, 2005), 54–55, 162.

Chapter 1: Spiritual Monarchs

1. I have adopted the present tense in reference to female spiritual monarchs and all activity in the spiritual invisible world. This is because the belief in these entities, as well as the power and authority that they hold, exists *still* in African communities.

2. Emeka C. Ekeke and Chike A. Ekeopara, "God, Divinities, and Spirits in African Traditional Religious Ontology," *American Journal of Social and Management Sciences* 1, no. 2 (2010): 213.

3. Ekeke and Ekeopara, 213.

4. Musa W. Dube, "Postcolonial Feminist Perspectives on African Religions," in *The Wiley-Blackwell Companion to African Religions,* ed. Elias Kifon Bongmba (Malden, MA: Blackwell, 2012), 134.

5. Ekeke and Ekeopara, "God, Divinities, and Spirits," 213.

6. Ekeke and Ekeopara, 213.

7. Ekeke and Ekeopara, 213.

8. Peter J. Paris, *The Spirituality of African Peoples: The Search for a Common Moral Discourse* (Minneapolis, MN: Fortress Press, 1995), 29.

9. Kodjo Amedjorteh Senah, *Money Be Man: The Popularity of Medicines in a Rural Ghanaian Community* (Amsterdam: Het Spinhuis, 1997), 86.

10. Dube, "Postcolonial Feminist Perspectives on African Religions," 134.

11. Dube, 134.

12. Geoffrey Parrinder, *Religion in Africa* (Harmondsworth, UK: Penguin, 1969), 46; emphasis added.

13. Nisbet Taisekwa Taringa, "African Metaphors for God: Male or Female?" *Scriptura* 86 (2004): 177.

14. Taringa, 176.

15. Taringa, 177.

16. The *tangena* is an indigenous tree distinguished by the high toxicity of its nuts, which have historically been used for trials by ordeal in Madagascar.

17. James Sibree, ed., "Tanala Customs, Superstitions, and Beliefs," in *The Antananarivo Annual and Madagascar Magazine,* vols. 1–2 (Antananarivo, Madagascar: Printed at the Press of the London Missionary Society, 1875), 97.

18. Robert M. Baum, *Shrines of the Slave Trade: Diola Religion and Society in Precolonial Senegambia* (Oxford: Oxford University Press, 1999), 39.

19. Baum, 39.

20. Walter E. A. van Beek et al., "Dogon Restudied: A Field Evaluation of the Work of Marcel Griaule [and Comments and Replies]," *Current Anthropology* 32, no. 2 (1991): 146.

21. Laird Scranton, "Amma," in *Encyclopedia of African Religion,* ed. Molefi Kete Asante and Ama Mazama (Los Angeles, CA: Sage Publications, 2009), 40–41.

22. Lesley Stevens, "Religious Change in a Haya Village, Tanzania," *Journal of Religion in Africa/Religion en Afrique* 21 (1991): 6.

23. Rudolf Anthes, "Egyptian Theology in the Third Millennium BC," *Journal of Near Eastern Studies* 18, no. 3 (1959): 169–212; Pierre Grimal, *Larousse World Mythology* (Secaucus, NJ: Chartwell Books, 1965), 32.

24. C. G. Seligman, "The Religion of the Pagan Tribes of the White Nile," *Africa: Journal of the International African Institute* 4, no. 1 (1931): 4.

25. Mimi Lobell, "Temples of the Great Goddess," in "The Great Goddess," special issue of *Heresies: A Feminist Publication on Art and Politics,* no. 5 (Spring 1978): 37.

26. Jonalyn Crisologo, *Egyptian Mythology: Ancient Gods and Goddesses of the World* (Mendon, UT: Mendon Cottage Books, 2014), 26–30.

27. Walter Addison Jayne, *Healing Gods of Ancient Civilizations* (Whitefish, MT: Kessinger Publishing, 2003).

28. Burleigh Muten, *Goddesses: A World of Myth and Magic* (Cambridge, MA: Barefoot Books, 2003).

29. Akan Takruri, *100 African Religions before Slavery and Colonization* (N.p.: Jamal White, 2017), 273.

30. Carolee Thea, "Masks, Power and Sisterhood in African Society," in "The Great Goddess, special issue of *Heresies: A Feminist Publication on Art and Politics*, no. 5 (1978): 110; Nefer Nika Miller-Herew, *Oshun the River Goddess* (CreateSpace Independent Publishing Platform, 2015).

31. Thea, "Masks, Power and Sisterhood in African Society," 106–11.

32. Suzanne Preston Blier, *African Vodun: Art, Psychology, and Power* (Chicago: University of Chicago Press, 1996), 33.

33. Blier, 33.

34. Fima Lifshitz, *An African Journey through Its Art* (Bloomington, IN: AuthorHouse, 2009), 63.

35. Lifshitz, 63.

36. Lifshitz, 63.

37. Muten, *Goddesses*.

38. Kathleen Sheldon, *African Women: Early History to the 21st Century* (Bloomington: Indiana University Press, 2017), 21.

39. Kenneth O. Dike and Felicia Ekejiuba, *Aro of Southeastern Nigeria, 1650–1980: Study of Socio-economic Formation and Transformation in Nigeria* (Ibadan: University Press, 1990).

40. Nwando Achebe, *Farmers, Traders, Warriors, and Kings: Female Power and Authority in Northern Igboland, 1900–1960* (Portsmouth, NH: Heinemann, 2005), 54–60.

41. E. Jensen Krige and J. D. Krige, *The Realm of a Rain Queen: A Study of the Pattern of Lovedu Society* (London: Oxford University Press, 1947), 12.

42. TimesLive, "State Recognises the Rain Queen," https://www.timeslive.co.za/news/south-africa/2016-05-30-state-recognises-the-rain-queen/ Accessed April 23, 2020.

43. Iris Berger, "Rebels or Status Seekers? Women as Spirit Mediums in East Africa," in *Women in Africa: Studies in Social and Economic Change,* ed. Nancy Hafkin and Edna G. Bay (Stanford, CA: Stanford University Press, 1976), 157–81.

44. Mambo Mupepi, *British Imperialism in Zimbabwe: Narrating the Organizational Development of the First Chimurenga (1883–1904)* (San Diego, CA: Cognella Academic Publishing, 2014).

45. Susan Schuster Campbell, *Called to Heal: African Shamanic Healers* (Detroit: Lotus Press, 1998).

46. J. Leclant, "The Civilization of Napata and Meroe," in *UNESCO General History of Africa,* Vol. II, ed. Muḥammad Jamāl al-Dīn Mukhtār (London: James Currey, 1986), 174.

47. Anthony Ephirim-Donkor, *African Spirituality: On Becoming Ancestors,* rev. ed. (Lanham, MD: University Press of America, 2011), 61.

48. Elizabeth Colson, "A Continuing Dialogue: Prophets and Local Shrines among the Tonga of Zambia," in *Religious Cults,* ed. Richard P. Werbner (New York: Academic Press, 1977), 119–37.

49. Parrinder, *Religion in Africa,* 58–59.

50. Kofi Appiah-Kubi, *Man Cures, God Heals: Religion and Medical Practice among the Akans of Ghana* (Totowa, NJ: Allanheld, Osmun, 1981), 20–24.

51. Robert Baum, *West Africa's Women of God: Alinesitoué and the Diola Prophetic Tradition* (Bloomington: Indiana University Press, 2015), 124–84.

Chapter 2: Queens, Queen Mothers, Princesses, and Daughters

1. The Lovedu rain queens of Southern Africa and the Mende paramount chiefs of West Africa seem to be exceptions to this rule.

2. Sandra T. Barnes, "Gender and the Politics of Support and Protection in Precolonial West Africa," in *Queens, Queen Mothers, Priestesses, and Power: Case Studies in African Gender,* ed. Flora Edouwaye S. Kaplan, *Annals of the New York Academy of Sciences* 810, no. 1 (1997): 2, https://doi.org/10.1111 /j.1749-6632.1997.tb48122.x.

3. I use the term *classificatory mother* to reference a woman who fills the role of mother but is not a birth mother.

4. Marianne Eaton-Krauss, "Encore: The Coffins of Ahhotep, the Wife of Seqeni-en-Re Tao and Mother of Ahmose," in *Ägypten-Münster,* ed. E. Graefe et al. (Wiesbaden, Germany: Otto Harrassowitz, 2003), 75–89.

5. David Sweetman, *Women Leaders in African History* (Portsmouth, NH: Heinemann Educational Books, 1984), 9.

6. Carolyn Fluehr-Lobban, "Nubian Queens in the Nile Valley and Afro-Asiatic Cultural History," a paper presented at the Ninth International Conference for Nubian Studies, Museum of Fine Arts, Boston, August 20–26, 1998, 2.

7. P. L. Shinnie, *Meroë: A Civilization of the Sudan* (New York: Praeger, 1967).

8. Regnant kandakes are kandakes who ruled in their own right.

9. Fluehr-Lobban, "Nubian Queens," 2.

10. *Mfecane* (Zulu), *Difaqane* or *Lifaqane* (Sesotho), literally, crushing, scattering, forced dispersal, forced migration, is used to reference a period (1815–40) of widespread chaos and warfare among the indigenous nations residing in the present-day country of South Africa.

11. Scott Rosenberg and Richard F. Weisfelder, *Historical Dictionary of Lesotho* (Plymouth, MA: Scarecrow Press, 2013), 302.

12. Bolanle Awe, "The Institution of the Iyalode within the Traditional Yoruba Political System," presented at the Seventeenth Annual Meeting of the African Studies Association, Chicago, October 30–November 2, 1974.

13. Jessica Amanda Salmonson, *The Encyclopedia of Amazons: Women Warriors from Antiquity to the Modern Era* (New York: Open Road Media, 2015).

14. Mahdi Adamu, *The Hausa Factor in West African History* (London: Oxford University Press, 1979), 4, 50.

15. Walter Gam Nkwi, *Voicing the Voiceless: Contributions to Closing Gaps in Cameroon History, 1958–2009* (Mankon, Cameroon: Langaa Research and Publishing, 2010), 18–19.

16. Agnes Akosua Aidoo, "Asante Queen Mothers in Government and Politics in the Nineteenth Century," in *The Black Woman Cross-Culturally,* ed. Filomina Chioma Steady (Rochester, VT: Schenkman, 1982), 72–75.

17. A. Adu Boahen, *African Perspectives on Colonialism* (Baltimore, MD: Johns Hopkins University Press, 1987), 24.

18. Steven Mock, *Symbols of Defeat in the Construction of National Identity* (New York: Cambridge University Press, 2012), 136.

19. Beverly J. Stoeltje, "Asante Queen Mothers: A Study in Female Authority," in Kaplan, *Queens, Queen Mothers, Priestesses, and Power,* 41–71.

20. Edna G. Bay, "The *Kpojito* or 'Queen Mother' of Precolonial Dahomey: Towards an Institutional History," in Kaplan, *Queens, Queen Mothers, Priestesses, and Power,* 9–40.

21. Iris Berger and E. Frances White, *Women in Sub-Saharan Africa: Restoring Women to History* (Bloomington: Indiana University Press, 1995), 75.

22. Thoko Ginindza, "Labotsibeni/Gwamile Mdluli: The Power behind the Swazi Throne 1875–1925," in Kaplan, *Queens, Queen Mothers, Priestesses, and Power,* 135–58.

23. Barnes, "Gender and the Politics of Support," 1–18.

24. Holly Hanson, "Queen Mothers and Good Government in Buganda: The Loss of Women's Political Power in Nineteenth-Century East Africa," in *Women in African Colonial Histories,* ed. Jean Allman, Susan Geiger, and Nakanyike Musisi (Bloomington: Indiana University Press, 2002), 219–22.

25. Vicki León, *Uppity Women of Medieval Times* (Berkeley, CA: Conari Press, 1997), 206.

26. Nwando Achebe, *The Female King of Colonial Nigeria: Ahebi Ugbabe* (Bloomington: Indiana University Press, 2011), 62–93.

27. Arnaud Zohou (dir.), *Hangbé, Forgotten Queen,* Peeping Tom Association, France, 2002, 87 minutes.

28. Maxwell Z. Shamase, "Princess Mkabayi Kajama of the Zulu Monarchy (c.1750–c.1843): Through the Keyhole of Oral History," unpublished paper, 1–14, https://www.academia.edu/8306256/PRINCESS_MKABAYI_KAJAMA_OF_THE_ZULU_MONARCHY_c.1750_c.1843_THROUGH_THE_KEYHOLE_OF_ORAL_HISTORY.

29. Salmonson, *Encyclopedia of Amazons,* M.

30. Barbara W. Olson, *Gondar, Ethiopia, 1971–1975: Guests in the Ethiopian Highlands and Children of Zemecha* (Bloomington, IN: AuthorHouse, 2011), 371–72.

31. Nwando Achebe, *Farmers, Traders, Warriors, and Kings: Female Power and Authority in Northern Igboland, 1900–1960* (Portsmouth, NH: Heinemann, 2005), 161–92.

1. George Brooks, "The *Signares* of St. Louis and Gorée: Women Entrepreneurs in Eighteenth-Century Senegal," in *Women in Africa: Studies in Social and Economic Change,* ed. Nancy Hafkin and Edna Bay (Stanford, CA: Stanford University Press, 1976), 19–44; Hilary Jones, *The Métis of Senegal: Urban Life and Politics in French West Africa* (Bloomington: Indiana University Press, 2013), 19.

2. Jones, *The Métis of Senegal,* 11, 42, 45.

3. Sandra T. Barnes, "Gender and the Politics of Support and Protection in Precolonial West Africa," in *Queens, Queen Mothers, Priestesses, and Power: Case Studies in African Gender,* ed. Flora Edouwaye S. Kaplan, *Annals of the New York Academy of Sciences* 810 (1997): 11.

4. Barnes, 8.

5. Saburi Biobaku, "Madame Tinubu," in *Eminent Nigerians of the Nineteenth Century,* ed. K. O. Dike (Cambridge: Cambridge University Press, 1960), 33–41; Oladipo Yemitan, *Madame Tinubu: Merchant and King-Maker* (Ibadan, Nigeria: University Press, 1987).

6. Felicia Ekejiuba, "Omu Okwei, the Merchant Queen of Ossomari: A Biographical Sketch," *Journal of the Historical Society of Nigeria* 3, no. 4 (June 1967): 633–46.

7. Gracia Clark, *Onions Are My Husband: Survival and Accumulation by West African Market Women* (Chicago: University of Chicago Press, 1995), 251–53.

8. Gracia Clark, *African Market Women: Seven Life Stories from Ghana* (Bloomington: Indiana University Press, 2010), 149.

9. UC-Berkeley School of Information, "Beyond Market Prices: Mobile Phones in Trade and Livelihood Activities—Ghana, Uganda, India, China: accessed March 7, 2018, https://markets.ischool.berkeley.edu/profiles/plantain-wholesaler-and-market-queen-ghana/.

10. "Plantain Wholesaler and Market Queen, Ghana."

11. UC-Berkeley School of Information, "Beyond Market Prices: Mobile Phones in Trade and Livelihood Activities—Ghana, Uganda, India, China: Cloth Seller, Makola Mar-

ket, Accra, Ghana," accessed March 7, 2018, https://markets
.ischool.berkeley.edu/profiles/cloth-seller-ghana/.

12. James Brooke, "West African Women: Political Inroads," *New York Times,* August 10, 1987, http://www.nytimes
.com/1987/08/10/world/west-african-women-political
-inroads.

13. Lena Kohr, "Mama Benz, and the Taste of Money: A
Critical View of the 'Homespun' Rags-to-Riches Story of
Post-independent Africa," in *On the Edges of Development:
Cultural Interventions,* ed. Kum-Kum Bhavnani, John Foran,
Priya Kurian, and Debashish Munshi (New York: Routledge,
2009), 167–78.

14. Christine Dieterich, Dalia Hakura, and Monique Newiak, "In the Driver's Seat," *International Monetary Fund—
Finance and Development* 53, no. 2 (2016). http://www.imf.org
/external/pubs/ft/fandd/2016/06/dieterich.htm; "The Rise of
Female African Entrepreneurs," *Credit Suisse,* August 7, 2015,
https://www.credit-suisse.com/corporate/en/articles/news
-and-expertise/the-fabric-of-success-201508.

15. Ebbe Prag, "Women Leaders and a Sense of Power:
Clientelism and Citizenship at Dantokpa Market in Cotonou,
Benin," in *Africa's Informal Workers: Collective Agency, Alli-
ances and Transnational Organizing in Urban Africa,* ed. Ilda
Lourenço-Lindell (London: Zed Books, 2013).

Chapter 4: *Female* Headmen, Kings, and Paramount Chiefs

1. J. Tyldesley, *Chronicle of the Queens of Egypt* (London:
Thames and Hudson, 2006), 63.

2. Tyldesley, 63.

3. Jessica Amanda Salmonson, *The Encyclopedia of Amazons: Women Warriors from Antiquity to the Modern Era* (New
York: Open Road Media, 2015).

4. James Henry Breasted, *A History of the Ancient Egyptians*
(New York: Charles Scribner's Sons, 1905), 217.

5. Kara Cooney, *The Woman Who Would Be King: Hatshepsut's Rise to Power in Ancient Egypt* (Danvers, MA: Broadway
Books, 2015).

6. Nwando Achebe, *The Female King of Colonial Nigeria: Ahebi Ugbabe* (Bloomington: Indiana University Press, 2013), 62–63.

7. Harry N. K. Odamtten, "Dode Akabi: A Reexamination of the Oral and Textual Narrative of a 'Wicked' Female King," *Journal of Women's History* 27, no. 3 (Fall 2015): 61–85.

8. John K. Thornton, *Central Africans, Atlantic Creoles, and the Making of the Americas, 1580–1660* (Cambridge: Cambridge University Press, 2007).

9. Emmanuel Kwaku Akyeampong and Henry Louis Gates, Jr., *Dictionary of African Biography,* Vol. 1, *Abach–Brand* (Oxford: Oxford University Press, 2012), 2888–89.

10. Achebe, *The Female King of Colonial Nigeria.*

11. Akyeampong and Gates, *Dictionary of African Biography,* 1:2500–501.

Chapter 5: African Women Today

1. Dorcas Ettang, "Female Presidents in Africa: New Norms in Leadership or Reflection of Current Practice," in *Leadership in Postcolonial Africa,* ed. B. G. Jallow, Palgrave Studies in African Leadership (New York: Palgrave Macmillan, 2014), 189–210; OMGVoice, "11 African Female Presidents Who Will Inspire the Hell out of You," accessed March 7, 2018, https://omgvoice.com/lifestyle/inspirational-african-presidents/; Wikipedia, "List of Elected and Appointed Female Heads of State and Government," accessed March 10, 2018, https://en.wikipedia.org/wiki/List_of_elected_and_appointed_female_heads_of_state_and_government.

2. Laurel Wamsley, "Ethiopia Gets Its 1st Female President," National Public Radio, October 25, 2018, https://www.npr.org/2018/10/25/660618139/ethiopia-gets-its-first-female-president.

3. Inter-Parliamentary Union, "Percentage of Women in National Parliaments—Ranking as of 1st January 2020," IPU Parline: Global Data on National Parliaments, https://data.ipu.org/women-ranking?month=1&year=2020. At the time of that count, Sudan and Eritrea were not included in the rankings.

Sudan was suspended from the IPU when its parliament was dissolved following the coup d'état in April 2019; at that point, it had ranked 59th. Eritrea's election results were unavailable on January 1, 2020; on December 1, 2019, it ranked 89th.

4. See Algerian Press Service Online (APS Online), "President Tebboune Appoints New Government Members," accessed April 4, 2020, http://www.aps.dz/en/algeria/32555-president -tebboune-appoints-new-government-members.

5. See Inter-Parliamentary Union Reports on Angola, Benin, Botswana, Burkina Faso, Burundi, all accessed March 10, 2018: "ANGOLA: Assembleia nacional (National Assembly)," http:// archive.ipu.org/parline-e/reports/2007_A.htm; "BENIN As- semblée nationale (National Assembly)," http://archive.ipu .org/parline-e/reports/2033_A.htm; "BOTSWANA: National Assembly," http://archive.ipu.org/parline-e/reports/2041_A .htm; "BURKINA FASO: Assemblée nationale (National As- sembly)," http://archive.ipu.org/parline-e/reports/2047_A .htm; "BURUNDI: Inama Nshingamateka (National Assem- bly)," http://archive.ipu.org/parline-e/reports/2049_A.htm.

6. Paul Schemm, "In Ethiopian Leader's New Cabinet, Half the Ministers Are Women," *Washington Post*, October 16, 2018, https://www.washingtonpost.com/world/africa/ethiopias -reformist-leader-inaugurates-new-cabinet-half-of-the -ministers-women/2018/10/16/b5002e7a-d127-11e8 -b2d2-f397227b43f0_story.html?noredirect=on&utm _term=.4304a405ed0a.

7. Aili Tripp, Colleen Lowe Morna, and Dior Konaté, "Elec- toral Gender Quotas: Sub-Saharan Africa," in *Women, Quotas and Politics,* ed. Drude Dahlerup (London: Routledge. 2006), 112–37.

8. See Bureau of Democracy, Human Rights and Labor, *International Religious Freedom Report for 2016,* "Madagas- car" and "São Tomé and Príncipe," U.S. Department of State, accessed March 17, 2018, https://www.state.gov/j/drl/rls/irf /religiousfreedom/index.htm?dlid=148715&year =2010#wrappr.

9. It is my contention that the number of practitioners of indigenous African religions in Africa reported in fact books

such as the U.S. Department of State's *International Religious Freedom* is grossly underestimated. This is because the majority of Africans practice traditional African indigenous religions in syncretism with Christianity and/or Islam, and most likely will not report themselves as practicing indigenous African religions.

10. The Fountain of Life Church, accessed March 15, 2018, www.tfolc.org.

11. *Daily Media Nigeria,* "Who Is Faith Abiola Oyedepo? Biography/Profile/History of Wife of the Founder of Living Faith Church (AKA Winners Chapel) Faith Abiola Oyedepo," June 21, 2016, https://dailymedia.com.ng/faith-abiola-oyedepo-biographyprofilehistory-wife-founder-living-faith-church-aka-winners-chapel-faith-oyedepo/; Faith Abiola Oyedepo official website, "Faith Abiola Oyedepo—Giving Hope to Humanity," accessed March 16, 2018, http://faithoyedepo.org.

12. Funke Felix-Adejumo Foundation, "About Funke Felix-Adejumo," accessed March 17, 2018, http://www.funkefelixadejumo.org/about-funke-felix-adejumo/.

13. *De Champions League* (blog), "My Life Is Story of Grace: Funke Adetuberu," October 11, 2013, http://dechampionsyouth.blogspot.com/2013/10/my-life-is-story-of-grace-funke.html.

14. "Adelaide Heward-Mills" (podcast), http://adelaidehewardmills.podbean.com; "Adelaide Heward-Mills," Dag Heward-Mills Ministries, https://www.daghewardmills.org/dhm/index.php/about-us/adelaide-heward-mills (both sites accessed March 16, 2018).

15. BBC News, "Ellinah Wamukoya Becomes Africa's First Anglican Woman Bishop," BBC.com, November 20, 2012, http://www.bbc.com/news/world-africa-20408199.

16. Anglican Communion News Service, "Second Female Anglican Bishop Elected by Southern Africa," *Anglican Journal,* October 9, 2012, https://www.anglicanjournal.com/articles/second-female-anglican-bishop-elected-by-southern-africa-11219/.

17. George Conger, "First Woman Bishop for GAFCON Province," *Anglican Ink,* February 3, 2018, http://anglican.ink/article/first-woman-bishop-gafcon-province.

18. "Pastor, Rev Kathy Kiuna Biography, Songs, Family, Children and House," Softkenya.com, December 20, 2014, https://softkenya.com/kenya/kathy-kiuna/.

19. "Rev Teresia Wairimu Biography, Age, Daughter, Family, Prophecy, Wealth and Social Media," Softkenya.com, December 28, 2015, updated October 16, 2019. https://softkenya.com/kenya/teresia-wairimu/.

20. Houssain Kettani, "Muslim Population in Africa," *Proceedings of the International Conference on Social Sciences and Humanities,* Singapore, October 9–11, 2009, accessed March 17, 2018, https://www.researchgate.net/publication/242523040_Muslim_Population_in_Africa.

21. See, for instance, Women Living Under Muslim Laws (WLUML), http://www.wluml.org; Egyptian Feminist Union (EFU); Muslim Women's Action Group in Kenya; Federation of Muslim Women's Associations (FOMWAN) in Nigeria; Grassroots Health Organization of Nigeria (GHON); Federal Organization of Muslim Women in Ghana (FOMWAG); Enterprising Women in Development (EWID); Tanzanian Muslim Council (BAKWATA); and Sahiba Sisters, Tanzania, to name but a few.

22. Beverly B. Mack and Jean Boyd, *One Woman's Jihad: Nana Asma'u, Scholar and Scribe* (Bloomington: Indiana University Press, 2000).

23. Alessandra Vianello, "Dada Masiti," in *Dictionary of African Biography,* ed. Emmanuel K. Akyeampong and Henry Louis Gates, Jr. (Oxford: Oxford University Press, 2011), 150–51.

24. Steve Esomba, *Wall Streets Infected by Arab Spring* (Morrisville, NC: Lulu Press, 2012), 42–43.

25. Sally Williams, "Mourchidat: Morocco's Female Muslim Clerics," *Telegraph,* April 26, 2008, https://www.telegraph.co.uk/culture/3672924/Mourchidat-Moroccos-female-Muslim-clerics.html.

26. Vanessa Rivera De La Fuente, "Recalling the Courage of Shamima Shaikh," Feminism and Religion, May 27, 2017, https://feminismandreligion.com/2017/05/27/shamima-shaikh/.

27. MasterCard Index of Women Entrepreneurs 2018, "Celebrating International Women, Empowering Women and Girls across Africa," accessed March 17, 2018, http://www .mastercard.africa.com.

28. AFP, "Isabel dos Santos May Lose Top Job in Angola's Unitel," News24, January 27, 2020, https://www.news24.com /Africa/News/isabel-dos-santos-may-lose-top-job-in-angolas -unitel-20200127; "Profile: Isabel dos Santos," Forbes, updated February 12, 2020, https://www.forbes.com/profile /isabel-dos-santos/.

29. "Profile: Folorunsho Alakija," Forbes, updated January 14, 2020, https://www.forbes.com/profile/folorunsho-alakija/.

30. Lionesses of Africa (blog), "Sibongile Sambo—The Startup Story of South Africa's Pioneering Female Aviation Entrepreneur," May 28, 2014, http://www.lionessesofafrica .com/blog/2014/5/28/sibongile-sambo-the-startup-story -behind-south-africas-pioneer-female-aviation-entrepreneur.

31. Mfonobong Nsehe, "Africa's Most Successful Women: Divine Ndhlukula," Forbes, January 20, 2012, https://www .forbes.com/sites/mfonobongnsehe/2012/01/20/africas-most -successful-women-divine-ndhlukula/#6124a1d75def.

32. "Profile: Aziz Akhannouch & Family," Forbes, updated February 12, 2020, https://www.forbes.com/profile/aziz -akhannouch/.

33. PulseLive KE, "Tabitha Karanja: Strength of a Woman: The Female CEO Running a Multi-billion Brewery," Business Insider by Pulse, May 30, 2017, http://www.pulselive.co.ke/bi /lifestyle/tabitha-karanja-strength-of-a-woman-the-female -ceo-running-a-multi-billion-brewery-id6757368.html.

34. "Women to Watch: Bethlehem Tilahun Alemu: Founder, soleRebels," Forbes, accessed March 17, 2018, https://www .forbes.com/special-report/2012/power-women/bethlehem -tilahun-alemu.html.

Bibliography

Achebe, Nwando. *Farmers, Traders, Warriors, and Kings: Female Power and Authority in Northern Igboland, 1900–1960.* Portsmouth, NH: Heinemann, 2005.

———. *The Female King of Colonial Nigeria: Ahebi Ugbabe.* Bloomington: Indiana University Press, 2011.

Achermann, Barbara, and Flurina Rothenberger. "The Rise of Female African Entrepreneurs." Credit Suisse, August 7, 2015. https://www.credit-suisse.com/about-us-news /en/articles/news-and-expertise/the-fabric-of-success -201508.html.

"Adelaide Heward-Mills" (podcast). http://adelaidehewardmills .podbean.com; "Adelaide Heward-Mills." Dag Heward-Mills Ministries. https://www.daghewardmills.org/dhm /index.php/about-us/adelaide-heward-mills. Both sites accessed March 16, 2018.

Aidoo, Agnes Akosua. "Asante Queen Mothers in Government and Politics in the Nineteenth Century." In *The Black Woman Cross-Culturally,* edited by Filomina Chioma Steady, 72–75. Rochester, VT: Schenkman, 1982.

Anglican Communion News Service. "Second Female Anglican Bishop Elected by Southern Africa." *Anglican Journal,* October 9, 2012. https://www.anglicanjournal .com/articles/second-female-anglican-bishop-elected -by-southern-africa-11219/.

Anthes, Rudolf. "Egyptian Theology in the Third Millennium BC." *Journal of Near Eastern Studies* 18, no. 3 (1959): 169–212.

Akyeampong, Emmanuel Kwaku, and Henry Louis Gates, Jr. *Dictionary of African Biography.* Vol. 1, *Abach–Brand*, 2888–89. Oxford: Oxford University Press, 2012.

Appiah-Kubi, Kofi. *Man Cures, God Heals: Religion and Medical Practice among the Akans of Ghana.* Totowa, NJ: Allanheld, Osmun, 1981.

Awe, Bolanle. "The Institution of the Iyalode within the Traditional Yoruba Political System." Paper presented at the Seventeenth Annual Meeting of the African Studies Association, Chicago, October 30–November 2, 1974.

Barnes, Sandra T. "Gender and the Politics of Support and Protection in Precolonial West Africa." In Kaplan, *Queens, Queen Mothers, Priestesses, and Power,* 1–18.

Baum, Robert M. *Shrines of the Slave Trade: Diola Religion and Society in Precolonial Senegambia.* Oxford: Oxford University Press, 1999.

———. *West Africa's Women of God: Alinesitoué and the Diola Prophetic Tradition.* Bloomington: Indiana University Press, 2015.

Bay, Edna G. "The *Kpojito* or 'Queen Mother' of Precolonial Dahomey: Towards an Institutional History." In Kaplan, *Queens, Queen Mothers, Priestesses, and Power,* 9–40.

BBC News. "Ellinah Wamukoya Becomes Africa's First Anglican Woman Bishop." BBC.com, November 20, 2012. http://www.bbc.com/news/world-africa-20408199.

Berger, Iris. "Rebels or Status Seekers? Women as Spirit Mediums in East Africa." In *Women in Africa: Studies in Social and Economic Change,* edited by Nancy Hafkin and Edna G. Bay, 157–81. Stanford, CA: Stanford University Press, 1976.

Berger, Iris, and E. Frances White. *Women in Sub-Saharan Africa: Restoring Women to History.* Bloomington: Indiana University Press, 1995.

Biobaku, Saburi. "Madame Tinubu." In *Eminent Nigerians of the Nineteenth Century,* by the Nigerian Broadcasting Corporation, 33–41. Cambridge: Cambridge University Press, 1960.

Blier, Suzanne Preston. *African Vodun: Art, Psychology, and Power.* Chicago: University of Chicago Press, 1996.

Boahen, A. Adu. *African Perspectives on Colonialism.* Baltimore, MD: Johns Hopkins University Press, 1987.

Breasted, James Henry. *A History of the Ancient Egyptians.* New York: Charles Scribner's Sons, 1905.

Brooke, James. "West African Women: Political Inroads." *New York Times,* August 10, 1987. http://www.nytimes.com/1987/08/10/world/west-african-women-political-inroads.html.

Brooks, George. "The *Signares* of St. Louis and Gorée: Women Entrepreneurs in Eighteenth-Century Senegal." In *Women in Africa: Studies in Social and Economic Change,* edited by Nancy Hafkin and Edna Bay, 19–44. Stanford, CA: Stanford University Press, 1976.

Bureau of Democracy, Human Rights and Labor. *International Religious Freedom Report for 2016:* "Madagascar" and "São Tomé and Príncipe." U.S. Department of State. Accessed March 17, 2018. https://www.state.gov/j/drl/rls/irf/religiousfreedom/index.htm?dlid=148715&year=2010#wrapper.

Campbell, Susan Schuster. *Called to Heal: African Shamanic Healers.* Detroit: Lotus Press, 1998.

Clark, Gracia. *African Market Women: Seven Life Stories from Ghana.* Bloomington: Indiana University Press, 2010.

———. *Onions Are My Husband: Survival and Accumulation by West African Market Women.* Chicago: University of Chicago Press, 1995.

Colson, Elizabeth. "A Continuing Dialogue: Prophets and Local Shrines among the Tonga of Zambia." In *Regional Cults,* edited by Richard P. Werbner, 119–39. New York: Academic Press, 1977.

Conger, George. "First Woman Bishop for GAFCON Province." *Anglican Ink,* February 3, 2018. http://anglican.ink/article/first-woman-bishop-gafcon-.

Cooney, Kara. *The Woman Who Would Be King: Hatshepsut's Rise to Power in Ancient Egypt.* Danvers, MA: Broadway Books, 2015.

Crisologo, Jonalyn. *Egyptian Mythology: Ancient Gods and Goddesses of the World.* Mendon, UT: Mendon Cottage Books, 2014.

Daily Media Nigeria. "Who Is Faith Abiola Oyedepo? Biography/Profile/History of Wife of the Founder of Living Faith Church (AKA Winners Chapel) Faith Abiola Oyedepo." June 21, 2016. https://dailymedia.com.ng/faith-abiola-oyedepo-biographyprofilehistory-wife-founder-living-faith-church-aka-winners-chapel-faith-oyedepo/.

De Champions League (blog). "My Life Is Story of Grace: Funke Adetuberu." October 11, 2013. http://dechampionsyouth.blogspot.com/2013/10/my-life-is-story-of-grace-funke.html.

De La Fuente, Vanessa Rivera. "Recalling the Courage of Shamima Shaikh." Feminism and Religion, May 27, 2017. https://feminismandreligion.com/2017/05/27/shamima-shaikh.

Dieterich, Christine, Dalia Hakura, and Monique Newiak. "In the Driver's Seat." *International Monetary Fund—Finance and Development* 53, no. 2 (2016). http://www.imf.org/external/pubs/ft/fandd/2016/06/dieterich.

Dike, Kenneth O., and Felicia Ekejiuba. *The Aro of South-eastern Nigeria, 1650–1980: Study of Socio-economic Formation and Transformation in Nigeria.* Ibadan: University Press, 1990.

Dube, Musa W. "Postcolonial Feminist Perspectives on African Religions." In *The Wiley-Blackwell Companion to African Religions,* edited by Elias Kifon Bongmba. Malden, MA: Blackwell, 2012.

Eaton-Krauss, Marianne. "Encore: The Coffins of Ahhotep, the Wife of Seqeni-en-Re Tao and Mother of Ahmose." In *Ägypten-Münster,* edited by E. Graefe et al., 75–89. Wiesbaden, Germany: Otto Harrassowitz, 2003.

Ekejiuba, Felicia. "Omu Okwei, the Merchant Queen of Ossomari: A Biographical Sketch." *Journal of the Historical Society of Nigeria* 3, no. 4 (June 1967): 633–46.

Ekeke, Emeka C., and Chike A. Ekeopara. "God, Divinities, and Spirits in African Traditional Religious Ontology." *American Journal of Social and Management Sciences* 1, no. 2 (2010): 209–18.

Ephirim-Donkor, Anthony. *African Spirituality: On Becoming Ancestors.* Rev. ed. Lanham, MD: University Press of America, 2011.

Esomba, Steve. *Wall Streets Infected by Arab Spring.* Morrisville, NC: Lulu Press, 2012.

Ettang, Dorcas. "Female Presidents in Africa: New Norms in Leadership or Reflection of Current Practice." In *Leadership in Postcolonial Africa,* edited by B. G. Jallow, 189–210. New York: Palgrave Macmillan, 2014.

Faith Abiola Oyedepo official website. "Faith Abiola Oyedepo—Giving Hope to Humanity." Accessed March 16, 2018. http://faithoyedepo.org/.

Fluehr-Lobban, Carolyn. "Nubian Queens in the Nile Valley and Afro-Asiatic Cultural History." Paper presented at Ninth International Conference for Nubian Studies, Museum of Fine Arts, Boston, August 26–28, 1998.

Funke Felix-Adejumo Foundation. "About Funke Felix-Adejumo." Accessed March 17, 2018. http://www.funkefelixadejumo.org/about-funke-felix-adejumo/.

Ginindza, Thoko. "Labotsibeni/Gwamile Mdluli: The Power behind the Swazi Throne 1875–1925." In Kaplan, *Queens, Queen Mothers, Priestesses, and Power,* 135–58.

Grimal, Pierre. *Larousse World Mythology.* Secaucus, NJ: Chartwell Books, 1965.

Hanson, Holly. "Queen Mothers and Good Government in Buganda: The Loss of Women's Political Power in Nineteenth-Century East Africa." In *Women in African Colonial Histories,* edited by Jean Allman, Susan Geiger, and Nakanyike Musisi, 219–22. Bloomington: Indiana University Press, 2002.

Idris, Hamza. "Women Arrest Boko Haram Fighters in Borno." *Daily Trust,* May 27, 2014. http://dailytrust.info/top-stories/25136-women-arrest-boko-haram-fighters-in-borno.

Inter-Parliamentary Union. Reports on Angola, Benin, Botswana, Burkina Faso, Burundi, all accessed March 10, 2018: "ANGOLA: Assembleia nacional (National Assembly)," http://archive.ipu.org/parline-e/reports/2007_A.htm; "BENIN Assemblée nationale (National Assembly)," http://archive.ipu.org/parline-e/reports/2033_A.htm; "BOTSWANA: National Assembly," http://archive.ipu.org/parline-e/reports/2041_A.htm; "BURKINA FASO:

Assemblée nationale (National Assembly)," http://archive
.ipu.org/parline-e/reports/2047_A.htm; "BURUNDI: Inama
Nshingamateka (National Assembly)," http://archive.ipu
.org/parline-e/reports/2049_A.htm.

———. "Percentage of Women in National Parliaments—
Ranking as of 1st January 2020." IPU Parline: Global Data
on National Parliaments. https://data.ipu.org/women
-ranking?month=1&year=2020.

Jayne, Walter Addison. *Healing Gods of Ancient Civilizations.*
Whitefish, MT: Kessinger Publishing, 2003.

Jones, Hilary. *The Métis of Senegal: Urban Life and Politics
in French West Africa.* Bloomington: Indiana University
Press, 2013.

Kaplan, Flora Edouwaye S., ed. *Queens, Queen Mothers, Priestesses, and Power: Case Studies in African Gender.* (*Annals
of the New York Academy of Sciences* 810.) New York: New
York Academy of Sciences, 1997.

Kettani, Houssain. "Muslim Population in Africa." *Proceedings
of the International Conference on Social Sciences and Humanities,* Singapore, October 9–11, 2009. Accessed March
17, 2018. https://www.researchgate.net/publication
/242523040_Muslim_Population_in_Africa.

Kohr, Lena. "Mama Benz, and the Taste of Money: A Critical
View of the 'Homespun' Rags-to-Riches Story of Post-
independent Africa." In *On the Edges of Development:
Cultural Interventions,* edited by Kum-Kum Bhavnani,
John Foran, Priya Kurian, and Debashish Munshi, 167–
78. New York: Routledge, 2009.

Krige, E. Jensen, and J. D. Krige. *The Realm of a Rain Queen:
A Study of the Pattern of Lovedu Society.* London: Oxford
University Press, 1947.

Krige, Jack, and Eileen Krige. *The Realm of a Rain Queen: A
Study of the Pattern of Lovedu Society.* KwaZulu, South
Africa: University of KwaZulu-Natal Press 1981.

Leclant, J. "The Civilization of Napata and Meroe." In
UNESCO General History of Africa, vol. 2, edited by
Muḥammad Jamāl al-Dīn Mukhtār. London: James Cur-
rey, 1986.

León, Vicki. *Uppity Women of Medieval Times.* Berkeley, CA: Conari Press, 1997.

Lifshitz, Fima. *An African Journey through Its Art.* Bloomington, IN: AuthorHouse, 2009.

Lionesses of Africa (blog). "Sibongile Sambo—The Startup Story of South Africa's Pioneering Female Aviation Entrepreneur." May 28, 2014. http://www.lionessesofafrica .com/blog/2014/5/28/sibongile-sambo-the-startup -story-behind-south-africas-pioneer-female-aviation -entrepreneur.

Lobell, Mimi. "Temples of the Great Goddess." In "The Great Goddess," special issue of *Heresies: A Feminist Publication on Art and Politics,* no. 5 (Spring 1978): 32–39.

Mack, Beverly B., and Jean Boyd. *One Woman's Jihad: Nana Asma'u, Scholar and Scribe.* Bloomington: Indiana University Press, 2000.

Mahdi Adamu. *The Hausa Factor in West African History.* London: Oxford University Press, 1979.

MasterCard Index of Women Entrepreneurs 2018. "Celebrating International Women, Empowering Women and Girls across Africa," accessed March 17, 2018. http:// www.mastercard.africa.com.

Miller-Herew, Nefer Nika. *Oshun the River Goddess.* CreateSpace Independent Publishing Platform, 2015.

Mock, Steven. *Symbols of Defeat in the Construction of National Identity.* New York: Cambridge University Press, 2012.

Mupepi, Mambo. *British Imperialism in Zimbabwe: Narrating the Organizational Development of the First Chimurenga (1883–1904).* San Diego, CA: Cognella Academic Publishing, 2014.

Muten, Burleigh. *Goddesses: A World of Myth and Magic.* Cambridge, MA: Barefoot Books, 2003.

Nkwi, Walter Gam. *Voicing the Voiceless: Contributions to Closing Gaps in Cameroon History, 1958–2009.* Mankon, Cameroon: Langaa Research and Publishing, 2010.

Nsehe, Mfonobong. "Africa's Most Successful Women: Divine Ndhlukula." *Forbes,* January 20, 2012. https:// www.forbes.com/sites/mfonobongnsehe/2012/01/20

/africas-most-successful-women-divine-ndhlukula
/#6124a1d75def.

Odamtten, Harry N. K. "Dode Akabi: A Reexamination of the Oral and Textual Narrative of a 'Wicked' Female King." *Journal of Women's History* 27, no. 3 (Fall 2015): 61–85.

Olson, Barbara W. *Gondar, Ethiopia, 1971–1975: Guests in the Ethiopian Highlands and Children of Zemecha.* Bloomington, IN: AuthorHouse, 2011.

OMGVoice. "11 African Female Presidents Who Will Inspire the Hell out of You." Accessed March 7, 2018. https://omgvoice.com/lifestyle/inspirational-african-presidents/.

Paris, P. J. *The Spirituality of African Peoples.* Minneapolis, MN: Fortress Press, 1995.

Parrinder, Geoffrey. *Religion in Africa.* Harmondsworth, UK: Penguin, 1969.

Pinecrest, John. "Pastor, Rev Kathy Kiuna Biography, Songs, Family, Children and House." Softkenya.com, December 20, 2014, updated October 16, 2019. https://softkenya.com/kenya/kathy-kiuna/.

———. "Rev Teresia Wairimu Biography, Age, Daughter, Family, Prophecy, Wealth and Social Media." Softkenya.com, December 28, 2015, updated October 16, 2019. https://softkenya.com/kenya/teresia-wairimu/.

Prag, Ebbe. "Women Leaders and a Sense of Power: Clientelism and Citizenship at Dantokpa Market in Cotonou, Benin." In *Africa's Informal Workers: Collective Agency, Alliances and Transnational Organizing in Urban Africa,* edited by Ilda Lourenço-Lindell. London: Zed Books, 2013.

"Profile: Aziz Akhannouch & Family." *Forbes,* updated February 12, 2020. https://www.forbes.com/profile/aziz-akhannouch/#98e7ad524d83.

"Profile: Folorunsho Alakija." *Forbes,* updated January 14, 2020. https://www.forbes.com/profile/folorunsho-alakija/.

"Profile: Isabel dos Santos." *Forbes,* updated February 12, 2020. https://www.forbes.com/profile/isabel-dos-santos/.

PulseLive KE. "Tabitha Karanja: Strength of a Woman: The Female CEO Running a Multi-billion Brewery." Business Insider by Pulse, May 30, 2017. http://www.pulselive

.co.ke/bi/lifestyle/tabitha-karanja-strength-of-a-woman
-the-female-ceo-running-a-multi-billion-brewery
-id6757368.html.

Rosenberg, Scott, and Richard F. Weisfelder. *Historical Dictionary of Lesotho.* Plymouth, MA: Scarecrow Press, 2013.

Salmonson, Jessica Amanda. *The Encyclopedia of Amazons: Women Warriors from Antiquity to the Modern Era.* New York: Open Road Media, 2015.

Schemm, Paul. "In Ethiopian Leader's New Cabinet, Half the Ministers Are Women." *Washington Post,* October 16, 2018. https://www.washingtonpost.com/world/africa/ethiopias
-reformist-leader-inaugurates-new-cabinet-half
-of-the-ministers-women/2018/10/16/b5002e7a-d127
-11e8-b2d2-f397227b43f0_story.html.

Scranton, Laird. "Amma." In *Encyclopedia of African Religion,* edited by Molefi Kete Asante and Ama Mazama, 40–41. Los Angeles: Sage Publications, 2009.

Seligman, C. G. "The Religion of the Pagan Tribes of the White Nile." *Africa: Journal of the International African Institute* 4, no. 1 (1931): 1–21.

Senah, Kodjo Amedjorteh. *Money Be Man: The Popularity of Medicines in a Rural Ghanaian Community.* Amsterdam: Het Spinhuis, 1997.

Shamase, Maxwell Z. "Princess Mkabayi Kajama of the Zulu Monarchy (c.1750–c.1843): Through the Keyhole of Oral History." Unpublished paper, 1–14, https://www
.academia.edu/8306256/PRINCESS_MKABAYI
_KAJAMA_OF_THE_ZULU_MONARCHY
_c.1750_c.1843_THROUGH_THE_KEYHOLE_OF
_ORAL_HISTORY.

Sheldon, Kathleen. *African Women: Early History to the 21st Century.* Bloomington: Indiana University Press, 2017.

Shinnie, P. L. *Meroë: A Civilization of the Sudan.* New York: Praeger, 1967.

Sibree, James, ed. "Tanala Customs, Superstitions, and Beliefs." In *The Antananarivo Annual and Madagascar Magazine,* vols. 1–2. Antananarivo, Madagascar: Printed at the Press of the London Missionary Society, 1875.

Stevens, Lesley. "Religious Change in a Haya Village, Tanzania." *Journal of Religion in Africa/Religion en Afrique* 21 (1991): 2–25.

Stoeltje, Beverly J. "Asante Queen Mothers: A Study in Female Authority." In Kaplan, *Queens, Queen Mothers, Priestesses, and Power,* 41–71.

Sweetman, David. *Women Leaders in African History.* Portsmouth, NH: Heinemann Educational Books, 1984.

Takruri, Akan. *100 African Religions before Slavery and Colonization.* N.p.: Jamal White, 2017.

Taringa, Nisbet Taisekwa. "African Metaphors for God: Male or Female?" *Scriptura* 86 (2004): 174–79.

Thea, Carolee. "Masks, Power and Sisterhood in African Society." In "The Great Goddess," special issue of *Heresies: A Feminist Publication on Art and Politics,* no. 5 (Spring 1978): 106–9.

Thornton, John K. *Central Africans, Atlantic Creoles, and the Making of the Americas, 1580–1660.* Cambridge: Cambridge University Press, 2007.

Tripp, Aili, Colleen Lowe Morna, and Dior Konaté. "Electoral Gender Quotas: Sub-Saharan Africa." In *Women, Quotas and Politics,* edited by Drude Dahlerup, 112–37. London: Routledge, 2006.

Tyldesley, J. *Chronicle of the Queens of Egypt.* London: Thames and Hudson, 2006.

UC Berkeley School of Information. "Beyond Market Prices: Mobile Phones in Trade and Livelihood Activities—Ghana, Uganda, India, China. Plantain Wholesaler and Market Queen, Ghana." Accessed March 7, 2018. https://markets.ischool.berkeley.edu/profiles/plantain-wholesaler-and-market-queen-ghana/.

———. "Beyond Market Prices: Mobile Phones in Trade and Livelihood Activities—Ghana, Uganda, India, China: Plantain Wholesaler and Market Queen, Ghana." Accessed March 7, 2018. https://markets.ischool.berkeley.edu/profiles/cloth-seller-ghana/.

van Beek, Walter E. A., et al. "Dogon Restudied: A Field Evaluation of the Work of Marcel Griaule [and Comments and Replies]." *Current Anthropology* 32, no. 2 (1991): 139–67.

Vianello, Alessandra. "Dada Masiti." In *Dictionary of African Biography,* edited by Emmanuel K. Akyeampong and Henry Louis Gates, Jr. Oxford: Oxford University Press, 2011.

Wamsley, Laurel. "Ethiopia Gets Its 1st Female President." National Public Radio, October 25, 2018. https://www.npr .org/2018/10/25/660618139/ethiopia-gets-its-first -female-president.

Wikipedia. "List of Elected and Appointed Female Heads of State and Government." Accessed March 10, 2018. https:// en.wikipedia.org/wiki/List_of_elected_and_appointed _female_heads_of_state_and_government.

Williams, Sally. "Mourchidat: Morocco's Female Muslim Clerics." *Telegraph,* April 26, 2008. https://www.telegraph.co .uk/culture/3672924/Mourchidat-Moroccos-female -Muslim-clerics.html.

"Women to Watch: Bethlehem Tilahun Alemu: Founder, soleRebels." *Forbes,* accessed March 17, 2018. https://www .forbes.com/special-report/2012/power-women /bethlehem-tilahun-alemu.html.

Yemitan, Oladipo. *Madame Tinubu: Merchant and King-Maker.* Ibadan, Nigeria: University Press, 1987.

Zohou, Arnaud, dir. *Hangbé, Forgotten Queen.* France: Peeping Tom Association, 2002. 87 minutes.

Index

Page numbers in italics refer to figures.

218

221